POISON IVY POISON OAK POISON SUMAC
and their relatives

by

Edward Frankel, Ph.D.

Drawings by
Anthony Salazar

THE BOXWOOD PRESS

Distributed by:

The Boxwood Press
183 Ocean View Blvd.
Pacific Grove, CA 93950
(408) 375-9110

ISBN: 0-940168-18-9

Cover design by Elaine Koppany

Frankel, Edward.
  Poison ivy, poison oak, poison sumac, and their relatives / by Edward
Frankel; drawings by Anthony Salazar.
     p.   cm.
  Includes index.
  ISBN 0-940168-18-9
  1. Toxicodendron — Control. 5. Anacardiaceae. I. Title.
QK495.A498F73   1991
583'.28—dc20
                                                                91-13518
                                                                CIP

Printed in U.S.A.

To my wife *Regina*

and

my grandson *Max*

PREFACE

BOTANICAL field experiences, over many years, with students and the public at large, called attention to the discrepancy between myths and what is actually known about Toxicodendrons in general and Poison Ivy, Poison Oak, and Poison Sumac in particular. Although most people from coast to coast are familiar with these plants, at least by name, and many have had personal contact with them, there is much confusion, superstition, and misinformation about their characteristics and the allergic reactions they cause.

To bridge the gap between fact and fiction this book was written for the general public in a nontechnical style, providing up-to-date information about these poisonous plants and their botanical relatives.

Affiliation with the New York Botanical Garden gave me access to a magnificent library and a huge herbarium; also a staff of professional botanists to whom I am deeply indebted for their contributions. I give special thanks to Dr. Rupert Barneby, Curator, botanist extraordinaire, for sharing information, suggesting and providing references, translating Latin names, phrases, and passages, and above all, making himself available at all times for consultations.

I wish to express my gratitude to Dr. Arthur Cronquist, Senior Scientist, who generously shared his wide botanical knowledge with me. I am grateful to John D. Mitchell, Honorary Research Assistant, author of *The Poisonous Anacardiaceae of the World* and co-author of *The Cashew and Its Relatives,* for reviewing sections of the manuscript and making invaluable suggestions.

I am indebted to Ms. Lothian Lynas, Reference Librarian at The New York Botanical Garden and her staff for providing gracious assistance and unlimited access to the immense collection of references in my search of the literature.

Thanks to Dr. Barry M. Jacobson, allergist, for reviewing and contributing to the chapters on the medical aspects of urushiol-induced dermatitis.

To Dr. Ralph Buchsbaum, zoologist, author of *Animals Without Backbones* and President of The Boxwood Press, who has been most encouraging and unfailing in giving excellent advice and assistance, my thanks.

My appreciation to Anthony Salazar, botanical illustrator and teacher of scientific ilustrations at The New York Botanical Garden, who made the line drawings for this book. His patience, cooperation, and expertise were invaluable.

It is to my wife, Dr. Regina Rumstein-Frankel, that I am most indebted not only for suggesting the idea of the book but spending countless hours as agent, proof-reader, critic, expediter, and general manager during the writing. She was a constant, encouraging and supportive helper from the inception to the publication of this book.

Edward Frankel

Yonkers, New York
Spring, 1991

CONTENTS

Native species of *Toxicodendron*

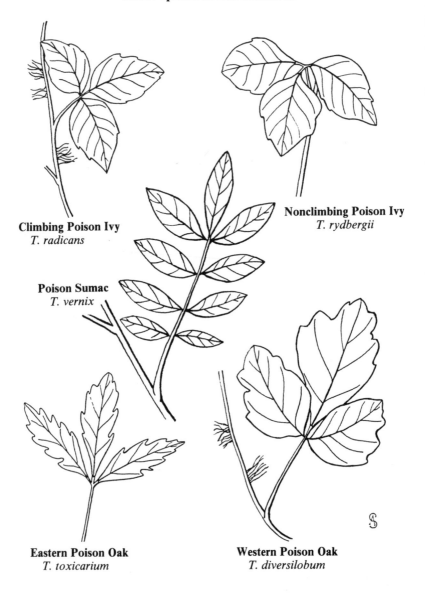

Climbing Poison Ivy
T. radicans

Nonclimbing Poison Ivy
T. rydbergii

Poison Sumac
T. vernix

Eastern Poison Oak
T. toxicarium

Western Poison Oak
T. diversilobum

Shapes of leaves in 5 native species of *Toxicodendron* found throughout continental United States except in Alaska and Nevada. Juices from these species are poisonous and capable of inflicting a mild to serious skin rash on susceptible individuals.

1

IS IT POISON IVY?

IN any public opinion poll, Poison Ivy would be voted the "most common," "most unpopular," and "most confusing" plant in the land. The very name Poison Ivy makes some people feel itchy, scratchy, and rashy. More than half the population in the United States has had some contact with this widespread weed at one time or another and to 3 out of 4 people, Poison Ivy is an anathema.

Despite its ubiquity and toxicity, a surprising number of individuals do not know this plant well enough to avoid it. Unwittingly, year after year, millions of people "shake hands" with this weed that leaves as its calling card an ugly, itchy, weeping, blistery rash. And to add insult to injury, most of the victims are at a complete loss to know how, when, and where they were "attacked." To make the situation more confusing, some individuals seem never to have experienced any unpleasantness with Poison Ivy—they are immune or, perhaps, have never touched the weed.

The rash usually surfaces a day or two after contact on hands, arms, feet, legs, face, or any other exposed part of the anatomy, depending upon the sufferer's state of undress while gamboling in the green. The rash runs its course for about a week or two, slowly subsides and disappears without a trace only to reappear the following year if the circumstances are similar.

What's in a name?

Poison Ivy shares the dubious distinction as a rash rouser with its botanical first cousins, Poison Oak and Poison Sumac. Poison Ivy and Poison Oak not only look very much alike but frequently grow side by side. Because of this strong resemblance, most folks use their common names interchangeably and indiscriminately. To rash victims, this distinction is academic since both cause the same misery. They declare:

> *What's in a name? That which we call Poison Ivy*
> *By any other name is just as venomous*

to paraphrase Juliet's immortal words to Romeo.

On the other hand, the name of the plant *is* important. The correct title indicates that you know the plant well enough to distinguish it from others. Anonymous herbs are faceless strangers, usually ignored or overlooked. To *know* Poison Ivy and its relatives by name is one way to remember to keep hands off these heinous herbs.

Common names

Unfortunately, a plant frequently has more than one common name. Poison Ivy has at least a dozen folk names in English (these to be sorted out later). In Canada, where Poison Ivy also grows, French-Canadians refer to it as "herbe a la puce," loosely translated as "herb of the flea" and "bois de chien" or "wood of the dog." The plant also flourishes in the Orient; the Chinese call it "tan chi" or "climbing vine" and the Japanese address it as "tsuta urushi," (oo-roo-she) or "climbing lacquer vine."

Common plant names have their place and value but have serious limitations particularly in communication between different regions of the same country and especially among people who do not share a common language.

Scientific names: binomials

Problems of communication created by multiple common names and language barriers were greatly reduced by the development of a system of scientific nomenclature. Each living thing has been given one and only one scientific name, which consists of two Latin or latinized words called a binomial. These two-word names are recognized and accepted by the scientific community internationally, although, as in most human enterprises, there is conflict among specialists over which names should be accepted.

This system of naming was introduced by the great Swedish botanist, Carl Linnaeus (1707-1779) about 250 years ago. It was designed to bring law and order to the confused, chaotic, unorganized nomenclatural methods of the times. Linnaeus remains the greatest nomenclator of all times, having baptized over 8,000 plants during his life. Most Linnaean binomials that have withstood the test of time and the barrage of botanical name changes may be recognized by the letter "L" that follows the binomial and stands for Linnaeus.

Binomial nomenclature

For a fuller understanding and appreciation of binomial nomenclature, one needs to be familiar with the present system of classification by which no less than half a million plants have been cataloged and named.

All living organisms are placed in one of 5 *kingdoms,* of which green plants is one. The *plant kingdom* consists of many divisions (or "phyla" in the animal kingdom; singular, "phylum"). A *division* of the plant kingdom contains a collection of classes. A *class,* in turn, is split into smaller units, orders. An *order* includes still smaller units, families. A *family* is broken down into genera (singular *genus).* A *genus* encompasses species. And a *species,* the basic unit of classification, refers to a population of similar organisms different from others and whose members produce fertile offsprings when mated.

The classification system can be compared to a set of books that we may call *The Encyclopedia of Living Things.* One volume represents the plant kingdom; the chapters are the divisions; pages are classes; paragraphs are orders; sentences, families; lines, genera, and words in the lines, species. Binomials (two names) consist of the genus designation followed by the species name.

Climbing Poison Ivy carries the label *Toxicodendron* (genus) *radicans* (species). Its original scientific name, *Rhus radicans,* still appears in botanical literature but is being replaced by modern scholars with its more recently adopted name *Toxicodendron radicans.* One reason for name changes is that scientists may find a group once considered homogeneous really consists of two (or more) kinds of plants because important details in the structure or function differ. On the other hand, descriptions of organisms once thought to represent two distinctive species have been found to be two growth forms or two stages in the development of a single species and so must be combined under a single species name.

It is conventional to italicize scientific names, and to capitalize the first letter of the genus name, followed by the species name or epithet, all in lower case letters. Also, when the binomial is repeated in the same discussion, the genus name is abbreviated to the first letter, e.g., *T. radicans.*

The story of this name change goes back to Linnaeus who lumped Poison Ivy, Poison Oak, and Poison Sumac with such nonpoisonous sumacs as Staghorn, Smooth, Winged (or Dwarf) in the same genus, *Rhus.* Thus, for over 200 years, *Rhus* was the first name of the toxic trio.

However, the accumulation of data from botanical exploration and research over the past two centuries pointed to significant differences between the poisonous and nonpoisonous sumacs. These findings led some botanists to have second thoughts about Linnaean nomenclature. By the 1930s, it was recommended that the nonpoisonous sumacs remain in the genus *Rhus* and the poisonous species be placed in a separate genus *Toxicodendron.* The name, which means "poisonous plant" (*toxico*, poison; *dendron,* plant or tree), aptly describes these herbs and is slowly being accepted by botanists in place of *Rhus.*

There have been other nomenclatural changes. Poison Ivy, formerly *Rhus radicans* L., is now split into *Toxicodendron radicans,* Climbing Poison Ivy, and *T. rydbergii,* Nonclimbing Poison Ivy. Poison Oak, formerly *Rhus toxicodendron* L., has also been divided into *T. toxicarium,* Eastern Poison Oak, and *T. diversilobum,* Western Poison Oak. Poison Sumac, previously *R. vernix* L. is now *T. vernix.* In short, the Linnaean toxic *Rhus* trio is now the *Toxicodendron* quintet— at least until further notice.

You may wonder why scientific names are in Latin, a dead language, one that most people either never studied or have long forgotten. During the middle ages Latin was the language of European scholars, the idiom in which they wrote and spoke, a tradition that persisted well into the 19th century. Scholarly works were seldom written in the vernacular, the native tongue, since this would limit the audience of readers and curtail intellectual exchange. Linnaeus, for example, whose mother tongue was Swedish, could communicate with botanists throughout Europe and America because he wrote and spoke Latin, which he was required to study during his training as a physician.

Proposing a scientific name for a plant to the botanical community is no simple matter. A standardized system of nomenclature published in the *International Code of Botanical Nomenclature* is followed by botanists worldwide. Rules for naming and establishing validity are spelled out based on the principle of priority of publication which states: For a "... binomial to be accurate and complete, and in order that the date may be readily verified, it is necessary to cite the name of the author(s) who first validly published the name concerned ... ."

New binomials appear, old ones disappear, and ancient ones reappear as botanists search for "first" nomenclators.

Armed with this minicourse in taxonomy and the "now" nomenclature, the reader is better prepared to follow the main characters in the tale of *Toxicodendron* and its botanical relatives.

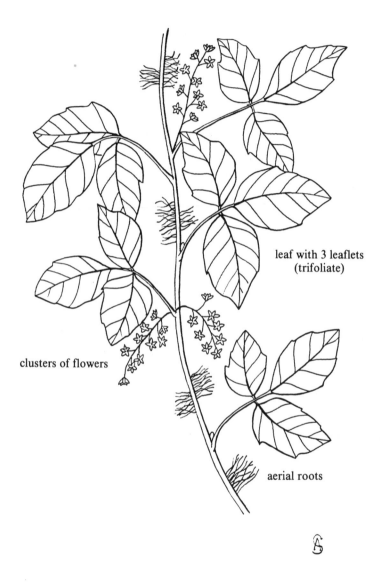

leaf with 3 leaflets
(trifoliate)

clusters of flowers

aerial roots

Climbing Poison Ivy *(Toxicodendron radicans)* showing trifoliate leaves, clusters of tiny greenish-white flowers, and aerial roots by which this vine clings and climbs.

2

CLIMBING POISON IVY

THE BEST KNOWN and the most feared in the genus *Toxicodendron* is Climbing Poison Ivy, *T. radicans*. As the most common and widespread species, the domain of this venomous vine stretches from southern Canada through the eastern part of the United States, down into Mexico, Central America, and on to Bermuda and the Bahama Islands. On the Atlantic seaboard it is most abundant on the rocky coast of New England and the sandbars of Long Island, New Jersey, and the Carolinas. It skips the west coast of the United States, but reaches across the Pacific Ocean into Taiwan, Japan, western and central China. The climbing (scandent) species is not native to any other part of the world, but where it has been introduced and cultivated it takes root and thrives.

Names, names, names

A plant with such a wide geographical distribution is bound to be known by a variety of common names and this is certainly true of *T. radicans*. Among its aliases are Common Poison Ivy, Cowitch, Three-Leaved Ivy, Poison Creeper, Climbing Sumac, Gift Sumac, Poison Oak, Markweed, Picry, Herbe a la Picry, and Poison Mercury. To this long list one could add other names based on personal experiences with this loathsome liana (vine) many of which may not be fit to print.

Often these common names are dramatic, descriptive, folk labels known locally and unknown elsewhere. The Orientals, as previously mentioned, have their own native names for this herb.

In the present scientific name of Climbing Poison Ivy, *T. radicans,* the species name *radicans* means "rooting" and refers to exposed hairlike structures, aerial roots, unique to this species, that cover the stem by which the vine climbs and clings.

Poison Ivy, people, and places

Climbing Poison Ivy is a "people plant." Where people go, Poison Ivy is sure to follow. As people multiply and spread out, so does Poison Ivy. It prospers in urban, suburban, and rural settings, in essentially disturbed areas: empty city lots, building grounds, along fences, hedges, utility poles, roadsides, river banks, and railroad embankments. As a climber, *T. radicans* creeps up walls, rocky cliffs, trees, shrubs, and the like. Parks, playgrounds, camp sites, golf courses, gardens, fields, meadows, woods, swamps, and bogs are invaded and occupied by this unwanted and uninvited intruder. As land is cleared or abandoned, new and old territories are opened to this aggressive squatter.

The Poison Ivy population seems to keep pace with the human population explosion. In all probability there are more members of this species today than in the past. Little wonder Poison Ivy has been dubbed "the most despised and most prolific weed" known to us.

A plant of many modes

Although there is a close association between people and Poison Ivy, this venomous vine too frequently goes undetected and therefore becomes a serious health hazard. A cogent reason for its anonymity is its ordinary, unspectacular appearance that blends with surrounding green vegetation. In addition, the lay person may be misled and confused by the diverse growth style and appearance of the species. Notwithstanding its common name, Climbing Poison Ivy, this plant also grows as a ground creeper, a short shrub, and sometimes as a small tree. All these growth modes may be observed within a small area. Such variations in life style add to the puzzlement of what is and what is not really Poison Ivy.

Leaflets three, turn and flee

Don't despair; don't throw yourself at the mercy of this wanton weed. There are several clues helpful in picking out

Poison Ivy in a lineup of possible perpetrators and distinguishing it from climbing, creeping, and shrubbing innocent companions. One of the best known aphorisms is "leaflets three, let it be" or for those who prefer to put distance between themselves and the suspect, "leaflets three, turn and flee."

These couplets of caution may be misleading and wrongly implicate harmless plants with 3 leaflets—trifoliates. Just remember:

> *It ain't necessarily so,*
> *It ain't necessarily so.*
> *Vines with leaflets three*
> *Poison Ivy be,*
> *It ain't necessarily so.*

There are several look-alike innocent trifoliates, easily mistaken for the real troublemakers. For example, strawberries, blackberries, and raspberries are trifoliates but their thorns and fruits exonerate them as people poisoners. Several trees and shrubs that often play host to viny ivy such as Bladdernut, Box-Elder, Wafer-Ash, and young Ash look suspiciously like Climbing Poison Ivy. They too are disqualified by virtue of their fruits and also as trees and shrubs. The prize imitators are Boston Ivy and Virginia Creeper. Both grow vines with trifoliate leaves although most of Boston Ivy leaves are 3-lobed and those of Virginia Creeper consist of 5 leaflets.

So far, the evidence seems to be that trifoliation is necessary but not sufficient to charge a plant as being Poison Ivy; more leads must be found.

Alternate leaf, possible grief

The second clue in tracking Climbing Poison Ivy is the position and the type of leaf on the stem. Leaves may grow in pairs, opposite one another, in whorls, or singly at different stem levels, that is, alternately. Buds and branches follow the same pattern as the leaves. Maples, ashes, and dogwoods follow an opposite pattern, whereas Poison Ivy and its kin assume the alternate format.

Harmless Trifoliates

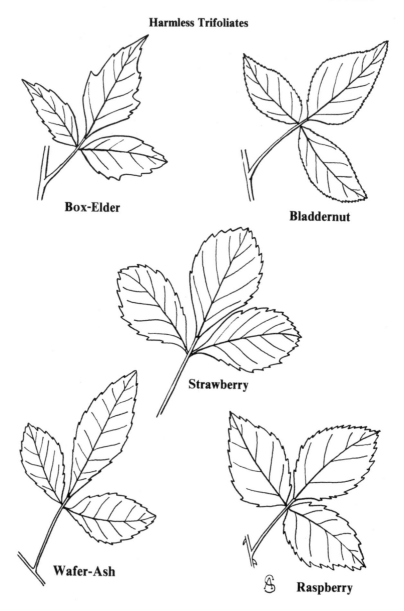

Box-Elder

Bladdernut

Strawberry

Wafer-Ash

Raspberry

Harmless trifoliates are often mistaken for Poison Ivy or Poison Oak because of their trifoliate leaves. The fruits distinguish them from harmful *Toxicodendron.*

Bladdernut. This common shrub has trifoliate leaves that may be mistaken for Poison Ivy. The fruit in the upper left is an inflated papery pod. (E.F.)

Box-Elder (Ashleaf Maple). This small tree is shown with trifoliate leaves that often resemble Poison Ivy. (E.F.)

The leaf type may be simple or compound. A leaf with or without lobes or indentations is a simple leaf. A compound leaf is composed of several separate leaflets which may be arranged palmately, like the fingers on your hand, or pinnately in a featherlike form with leaflets on either side of a common stem.

To see the difference between a leaf and a leaflet, look for the position of the bud. In a simple leaf, the bud is next to or under the base of the leaf stem, the petiole. In a compound leaf, the bud is at the base of the common stem and not at the base of the leaflet.

The 3 leaflets of Poison Ivy are arranged as follows: the middle or terminal leaflet is larger with a longer stem than the 2 side leaflets which are opposite one another. The ensemble resembles a 3-leaf clover plant.

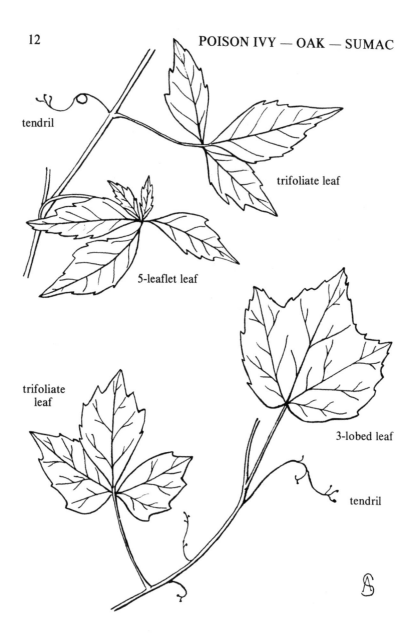

tendril

trifoliate leaf

5-leaflet leaf

trifoliate
leaf

3-lobed leaf

tendril

Virginia Creeper *(above)* has leaves with 3- and 5-leaflets, the latter more common. **Boston Ivy** *(below)* shows 3-leaflet (trifoliate) and 5-lobed leaves. Both are common vines that climb by tendrils and are easily mistaken for trifoliate Poison Ivy.

Leaf and Bud arrangements

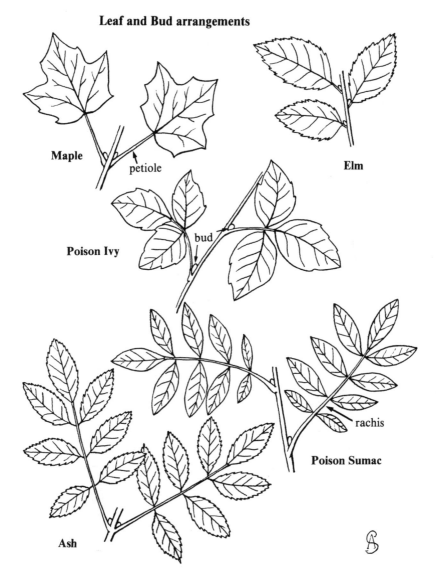

Poison Ivy and Poison Sumac display *alternate* leaf patterns, whereas Maple and Ash show *opposite* leaf arrangements. In addition, Poison Ivy and Poison Sumac, like **Ash**, are seen with compound leaves (more than one leaf on a stem) while **Maple** and **Elm** grow simple leaves. The position of the bud at the base of the leaf distinguishes between simple and compound leaves.

Thus, a vine bearing alternate trifoliate leaves should make you sit up and take notice but at arm's length. However, a vine fitting this description cannot be accused of being Poison Ivy beyond the shadow of a doubt. Additional evidence is needed and the search goes on.

Hairy vine, a danger sign

A third identifying mark clearly visible year round is *aerial roots,* short hairlike structures on the climbing stem of Poison Ivy. They first appear as reddish fuzz on the stems of young climbers; with age the aerial roots become more abundant and turn rust to grayish-black. The hairs secrete a powerful "glue" which firmly anchors the scaling stem to a tree trunk, a rocky wall, or any other vertical structure within reach.

Aerial roots of Climbing Poison Ivy in winter. Thick old stems are covered with dense growths of black aerial roots that attach the vine to a tree trunk. (E.F.)

Despite appearances, Poison Ivy vines are not parasitic; they climb and cling to other living plants for support and not sustenance. Sheer weight and extensive shading by the vine may smother or starve the host plant and so crush or kill it, all in quest for a place in the sun.

Cimbing vine, not so fine

The foremost feature of this climbing (scandent) species is the tendency to climb up vertical structures, dead or alive, almost anywhere but especially in areas disturbed by humans or natural forces such as floods, forest fires, and the like.

Favorite haunts of Poison Ivy are woodland borders and clearings that provide opportunities to exercise its prowess as climber. The vines are not fussy; they will mount almost any kind of tree or shrub but prefer those with vertically furrowed trunks affording them a rough surface for a firm grip and a climbing lane.

Green leafy vines may envelop the naked limbs of a dead tree so completely as to give it the appearance of a living Poison Ivy tree. The trunk of a living Elm may be clothed in green pantaloons fashioned from Poison Ivy vines and the leafy branches festooned with garlands of ivy creating the illusion of a hybrid Poison Ivy-Elm tree.

Most vines make their ascent in a spiral path either clockwise or counterclockwise. Poison Ivy rarely twines; it follows a straight and narrow path. Once the vine latches on to a tree, it will stay for years growing in height and breadth. With age the vines (lianas) resemble thick ropes lashed to tree trunks by myriads of blackish hairs.

Fences and walls of wood, stone, or metal are also frequented by these vaulting vines. It is fascinating to observe a Climbing Poison Ivy vine negotiating a chain link fence. The growing tip weaves in and out between the fence strands snaking its way up to the top where it appears to "reach out" in all directions "looking" for another ladder to climb. A fence sometimes serves as a support that enables the lower part of the vine to thicken to the point where the vine stands on its own and grows 10 to 20 feet as a true *Toxicodendron,* a Poison Ivy tree.

Sheer rock walls are no barrier but a challenge to this clinger. It climbs cliffs by aerial roots firmly glued to the stone surface. The ground around utility poles and fence rows is well populated by Poison Ivy due in part to the diet and toilet habits of perching birds.

Climbing Poison Ivy on a sheer rock wall. Note the trifoliate leaves. (E.F.)

Climbing Poison Ivy fruits, an avian delight, are picked from the vine and indigestible seeds are dropped below while sitting and socializing on wires and fences as birds are wont to do. Guano mixed with seeds provides fertile grounds for the propagation of new generations of Climbing Poison Ivy.

Climbing competitors

Climbing Poison Ivy competes with other equally aggressive upward strivers for a place on a prop. It is not unusual for *Toxicodendron radicans* to share a tree, post, or pole with other vining species. Among its climbing competitors are Virginia Creeper, Boston Ivy, Oriental Bittersweet, Moonseed, Grape, Climbing Hydrangea, Wintercreeper, and Porcelain berry—all woody vines and rugged rivals.

Oriental Bittersweet and Moonseed are twiners; with naked spiraling stems, they embrace one another as well as the objects of their affection, trees and shrubs. Porcelain berry and Grapes are tendril climbers that curl threadlike structures around twigs, wires, and trellises. Virginia Creeper and Boston Ivy cling by means of slender branching tendrils tipped with tiny disc-shaped adhesive pads. English Ivy, Climbing Hydrangea, and Wintercreeper are root climbers; they cement themselves by aerial roots similar to those of *T. radicans*. Regardless of how its competitors climb or cling, turn or twist, only Climbing Poison Ivy can boast of a hairy stem bearing alternate trifoliate leaves. This brings us one step closer to the suspect, the poisoning perpetrator. We can now add another line to our Poison Ivy poetry:

Hairy vine, a danger sign.

Fruit white, a warning sight

The most constant and reliable clues in tracking *Toxicodendron* in general and *T. radicans* in particular are the reproductive organs: flower, fruit, and seed. They are the bottom line of identification, the "essence" of the plant to quote Linnaeus. These structures are not as variable as leaves, stems, roots, growth patterns, and habitats.

Virginia Creeper clinging to a stone wall by branching tendrils *(upper left)*. Seen here is the more common 5-leaflet form; its 3-leaflet leaves, less common, are sometimes assumed to be Poison Ivy. (E.F.)

English Ivy climbs by aerial roots *(lower left)* similar to those of Climbing Poison Ivy and mistaken for it. (E.F.)

In June, Poison Ivy is in flower "busting out all over." This happening usually goes unnoticed since the petite Poison Ivy posies are partially hidden by the relatively large green trifoliate leaves. The flowers are bunches of unisexual 5-petaled, greenish-white, sweet-smelling blossoms along the length of the vine, axillary, that is, between the stem and the base of the petiole.

Most people never get close enough to see, let alone smell the flowers. At the sight of "leaflets three," they either "turn and flee" or "let it be." However, the more daring and curious discover that Poison Ivy vines are either male or female plants. The male vines bear flowers with stamens, the pollen-producing structure. Female vines are pistil-packing plants; each flower has a single pistil with a 3-parted style (the top of the pistil) and an ovary with an ovule containing the egg.

Bees, attracted by the sweet aroma and nectar of the staminate flowers, brush up against the tacky pollen powder which sticks to their hairy bodies. The pistillate vines are equally attractive to bees and in their quest for nectar, pollen-laden bees touch the tips of the triparted styles. In doing so, they perform the act of pollination; pollen is placed on the doorstep of the Poison Ivy egg in the ovary. In contrast to the noxious nature of the plant, its pollen and nectar are not toxic either to bees that collect these "goodies" or to humans that feast on the honey.

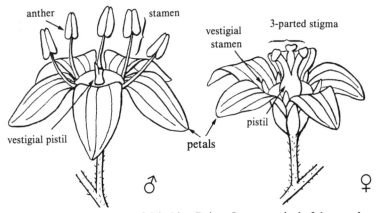

Male and female flowers of Climbing Poison Ivy are typical of the members of the genus *Toxicodendron*. They grow on separate vines in clusters along the stem above the base of the leaf. The male (staminate) flower is slightly larger than the female (pistillate). Both contain vestigial (nonfunctioning) reproductive organs of the opposite sex.

After landing on the tip of the pistil, each pollen grain grows a tube down into the ovary and ejects a sperm that fuses with the waiting egg. This fertilization ritual consumates the nuptial (wedding), thanks to the bees that minister the marriage.

By the end of June the male flowers, having fulfilled their sexual services as pollen providers, wither and die on the vine. Meanwhile, back in the ovary, a new generation of Poison Ivy is in the making. Clusters of fruits covered by a thin, dry, green skin, each containing a single seed, appear along the length of the female vine. These fruits are known botanically as drupes.

As the summer progresses, the green drupes ripen into pendulous bunches of small whitish fruits that may persist into the fall and winter unless birds get them first, which they usually do.

Don't be deceived by the birds and the bees that thrive on Poison Ivy flowers and fruits. For humans, the fruits are just as toxic as any other part of the plant. These dangerous drupes inspire the last caution:

Fruit white, a warning sight.

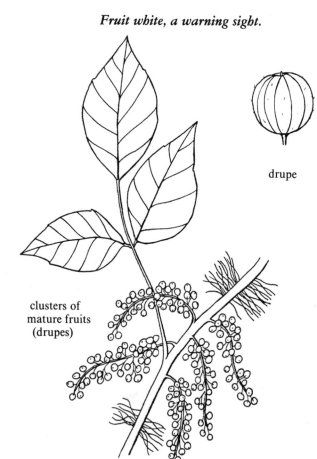

drupe

clusters of
mature fruits
(drupes)

Fruits of Climbing Poison Ivy. Thick clusters of waxy, whitish fruits (drupes) mature along the stem bearing female flowers. Each tiny drupe has distinct lines on the outer surface that may be covered with fine hairs.

Winter warning

By late fall and winter, when Climbing Poison Ivy is leafless and usually fruitless, only seemingly lifeless vines, creepers, and underground stems remain. Before coming to "grips" with unwanted "dead" ivy above and below the ground, look at the buds. A vine, stem or rhizome with alternate, fuzzy, stalked, and naked buds (no bud scales) is very likely Poison Ivy in its dormant winter stage. It is alive and well, waiting for the spring to leaf, flower, and fruit. Be advised that all parts of wintering Poison Ivy are full of poisonous sap just as potent as at any other time of the year and just as capable of inflicting a severe rash on susceptible individuals.

Woody perennials

A frequently overlooked feature of Climbing Poison Ivy and its kin is that they are woody plants, perennials, which live and grow from year to year like trees and shrubs. This species produces not only woody climbing stems as much as 75 feet in length and a circumference of 20 inches but also spreading

Woody stems of Climbing Poison Ivy, attached to a tree trunk, are each about 4 inches in diameter and about 10 years old. (E.F.)

Leaf variant of Climbing Poison Ivy. Leaflets with notched margins are less typical but not uncommon. (E.F.)

creeping stems, stolons, and branched horizontal underground stems, rhizomes. The underground rhizomes are also alternately budded and capable of rooting and growing into complete new Poison Ivy offsprings. This single-parent-inhouse method of asexual reproduction is faster and more dependable than the complicated sexual route of flowers, fruits, and fructification which is beholden to outsiders, bees for pollination and birds for seed dispersal.

A perplexingly variable species

Variety may be the spice of life but to botanists, amateur or professional, Climbing Poison Ivy is a problem plant, "a most perplexingly variable species." In addition to its diverse life style and habitat, the leaves of this species, its most familiar hallmark, are so variable that they can drive you to distraction. Not even trifoliation, the symbol of Poison Ivy, is sacred. Forms of the species are known in which the 2 side leaflets are missing and only the terminal center leaflet remains. Just imagine coming across the "impossible," a 1-leafed Poison Ivy plant. Populations with 4, 5, and as many as 17 leaflets have also been reported.

Leaflets may be slightly or deeply lobed, or entire, that is, neither lobed nor toothed. In texture, the foliage can vary from leathery thick to transparently thin, with a leaf surface that is rough or smooth, hairy or wooly. Mature leaflets may range in length from 2 to 8 inches or more. Some specimens grow leaflets a foot or more long and may well earn binomials, such as T. colossum, T. gargantuum, and T. giganteum.

Diverse leaf characteristics seem to be related to differences in habitat: growing in light or shade, in forests or fields, at various altitudes, with or without supports, and in dry or wet areas.

When experts declare T. radicans to be a nonconforming "perplexingly variable species" that gives them taxonomic troubles and headaches, one can appreciate the plight of the amateur who just wants to know which is and which is not Climbing Poison Ivy.

Less common variations in leaf shape of Climbing Poison Ivy.

3

NONCLIMBING POISON IVY

THIS SPECIES is known in the trade as *Toxicodendron rydbergii* in honor of Per Axel Rydberg (1850-1931), an expert on western flora. The species did not "exist" until the turn of the century when it was admitted to the genus as a full fledged member with all the rights and privileges thereof. Actually, *T. rydbergii* is a taxonomic spinoff from Climbing Poison Ivy, its closest botanical relative. For almost three centuries, this non-climber lived in the shade of its climbing cousin, *T. radicans,* as a subspecies or variety under names fashionable at the time. Although Linnaeus was aware of this nonclimbing plant, he did not award it species status and listed it as a variety of *T. radicans.*

Range of habitat

T. rydbergii enjoys a wide distribution and in the genus occupies the most northerly habitat. It is the only *Toxicodendron* species found in Canada from the Gaspé to the east side of the Cascade Mountains. Its range extends through-out the western United States, and isolated members of the species live on mountain tops in the Appalachians, possibly refugees from the last glaciers, 12,000 years ago.

Within its territory, *T. rydbergii* grows in practically every kind of ecological niche, usually in the company of *T. radicans* and other weedy plants. Seldom is it found in deep dark forests or heights above 4,000 feet. Its habitation is limited chiefly by lack of moisture and light.

Common names

As a recent arrival on the taxonomic scene, *T. rydbergii* has yet to earn its own common name. The lay person, unaware of its species status, sees "just plain Poison Ivy" and addresses it as such. Those in the know, botanists, refer to it as Rydberg's Poison Ivy, Canadian Poison Ivy, Northern Poison Ivy or Nonclimbing Poison Ivy. The latter name is preferred since it distinguishes the common climber from the northern non-climber.

Shrubby species

The main claim of *T. rydbergii* to specieshood is the lack of aerial roots. It stands on its stem as a subshrub and does not follow the clinging, climbing habits of its viny cousin. If undisturbed, this species can attain a height of 10 feet but generally is no more than a few feet tall. More commonly found in Canada, the boreal (northern) habitat differentiates *T. rydbergii* from *T. radicans.*

There are several other more subtle differences between these species. The nonclimber has larger and broader leaves, and larger and more tightly clustered fruits that are cream to yellow in color. To the amateur, such details are probably regarded as "nit picking" but to botanists they are important enough to justify the creation of new species and subspecies.

In all other respects, *T. rydbergii* displays traits typical of the genus: alternate, trifoliate leaves; unisexual axillary clusters of fragrant 5-parted flowers with 5 stamens in the male and one 3-parted style in the female; drooping clusters of yellowish drupes; spreading stolons, rhizomes, and poisonous sap.

Frequently, there is an overlap in the territories occupied by Climbing and Nonclimbing Poison Ivy with considerable inter-breeding between these very similar species. The resultant hybrids add to the taxonomic turmoil. In addition, the fact that not all members of *T. radicans* sprout aerial roots and hence do not climb, further compounds the confusion in classification.

For what little comfort it may bring to *Toxicodendron*-sensitive sufferers, *T. rydbergii* generally does not grow in southern New England, New York, and points south. This may be only of academic interest since its poisonous partner, *T. radicans,* backed up by Eastern Poison Oak, more than fills the gap.

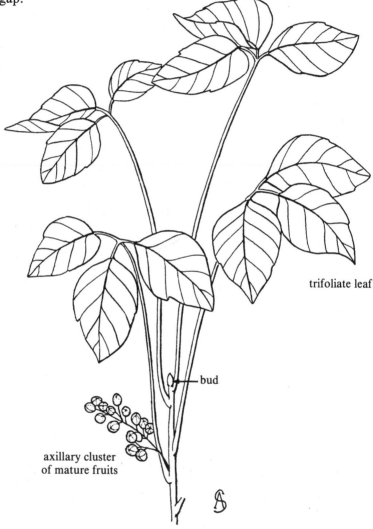

trifoliate leaf

bud

axillary cluster of mature fruits

Nonclimbing Poison Ivy *(Toxicodendron rydbergii)* is a more northerly species lacking aerial roots which distinguishes it from Climbing Poison Ivy *(T. radicans).* Hence it does not climb but grows as a short shrub. The trifoliate leaves tend to be spoon-shaped and clustered near the end of the branch. Flowers and fruits are very much like those of *T. radicans.*

4

POISON OAKS: EAST AND WEST

T HE THIRD MEMBER of the *Toxicodendron* troop is *T. toxicarium,* formerly known as *Rhus toxicodendron.* This less well-known species is an inhabitant of the sandy soil of the Atlantic and Gulf coast plains. Its domain extends from southern New Jersey to Florida and westward into parts of Texas and Oklahoma. The species is well established in shrub oak and pine forests in association with sandhill vegetation. The soil on which it grows is continuously drained coarse sand, very poor in mineral nutrients. Eastern Poison Oak prospers and reigns where other kinds of *Toxicodendron* can't make it.

The confusion of common names

No *Toxicodendron* has suffered more identity crises from multiple names than Eastern Poison Oak. Most folks call it Poison Ivy or any of its dozen aliases and leave it at that. As far as they are concerned this species looks and "stings" like Poison Ivy and they see no reason for giving it special nomenclatural consideration. Others, who note the oaklike leaflets, call it Oakleaf Poison Ivy or Oakleaf Ivy for short.

More confusion in scientific names

The present binomial for Eastern Poison Oak is *T. toxicarium,* a name recommended as recently as 1971. This new binomial is slowly gaining acceptance in some quarters of the international botanical community but is in competition with *T. pubescens,* an even more recently suggested binomial for Eastern Poison Oak.

For almost three centuries, this species ran the taxonomic gauntlet tagged with the Linnaean binomial *Rhus toxico-dendron,* a general utility label, applied freely and indiscrimi-

nately to the poison ivies and poison oaks. In fact, students of
the *Toxicodendron* genus describe its nomenclatural history as
"a mess"; the epithets *radicans* and *toxicodendron* have been
tossed back and forth between Poison Ivy and Poison Oak as a
"taxonomic tennis game."

At present, all is quiet on the Eastern Poison Oak front; *T.
toxicarium* has earned its stripes and name as a genuine species
in good standing. It is a legitimate bearer of the name *Toxicodendron* by virtue of its alternate trifoliate leaves, axillary
unisexual 5-parted flowers, single-seeded white to gray drupe
fruits, and rash-rousing sap.

The species' marks of distinction and uniqueness are fuzz-
covered leaves and fruits, leaflets that tend to have rounded tips,
no aerial roots, and its preference for a sandy soil habitat.
Lacking aerial roots, it is not viny as is *T. radicans* but a short
shrub like its northern relative *T. rydbergii* that it most resembles. Leaflets tend to be oak-shaped, a characteristic Eastern
Poison Oak shares with Western Poison Oak; leaflets are also
quite variable in size, shape, color, texture, edging, and lobing
and are therefore of limited value in identifying the species.
Briefly, the most reliable species diagnostics are a combination
of velvety appearance, subshrub life style, and sandy soil
habitation on the coastal plains of South Atlantic and Gulf
states.

Western Poison Oak: the pariah of the Pacific

If a plant could be banished by popular decree, no doubt
Western Poison Oak would be outlawed immediately by Pacific
coast residents. This species, the last of the native Toxicodendrons to be admitted to the botanical circle, now carries the
binomial *T. diversilobum*. The herb is strictly a Pacific coast
inhabitant. Its turf extends from southern British Columbia,
where it was first found, to Baja California, bordered on the east
by deserts, the Sierra and Cascade Mountains and on the west
by the Coastal Ranges. Within this region, *T. diversilobum* is

most hazardous and costly to human health due in part to its abundance as a woody shrub, particularly in the Golden State.

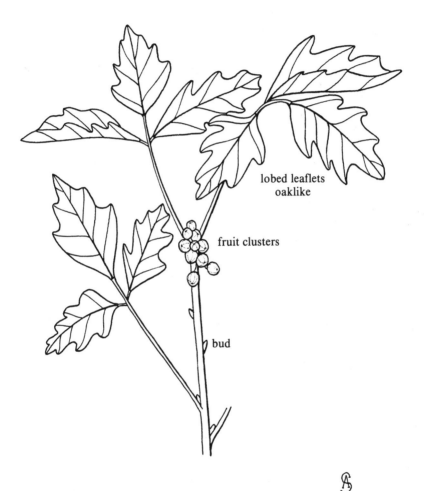

Eastern Poison Oak *(Toxicodendron toxicarium),* a southerly species without aerial roots, that grows as a short shrub. The branch shown has trifoliate leaves with leaflets that tend to have rounded lobes, some oaklike in appearance. Note the alternate leaves and buds. The fruits are drupes in axillary clusters, similar to those of Climbing Poison Ivy. Leaves and fruits are covered with a fine layer of hairs giving the plant a velvety appearance.

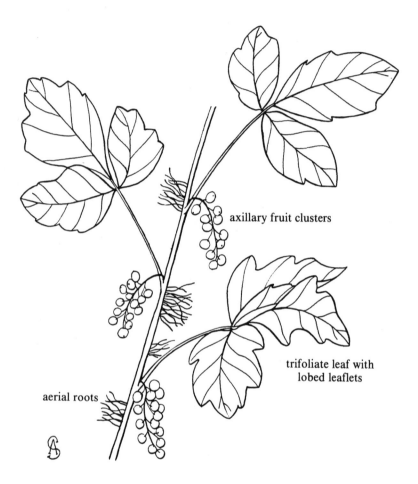

axillary fruit clusters

trifoliate leaf with
lobed leaflets

aerial roots

Western Poison Oak *(Toxicodendron diversilobum)* is strictly a Pacific coast species. Although it usually grows as a short shrub, aerial roots enable the plant to take the form of a vine. The leaves are trifoliate and the leaflets show great variation in lobing, some resembling oak leaves. Axillary clusters of fruits are much like those of eastern Toxicodendrons.

Names, names, names

Western Poison Oak was first discovered in 1830 on Vancouver Island in Canada by the British botanist David Douglas

(1799-1834) after whom the Douglas Fir tree is named. This new species was given botanical recognition as *Rhus lobata*. Since then, it has undergone several name changes in the hands of botanists and arrived at its present binomial *T. diversilobum* in 1905 and has kept that name ever since.

In addition to the label Western Poison Oak, there is no lack of common names; it answers to Pacific Poison Oak, Oakleaf Ivy, Yeara, and all other printable and unprintable names by which its eastern kith and kin are known.

History

Early white explorers and settlers who migrated north from Mexico encountered *T. diversilobum* along the way and called it "yiedra," the Spanish word for ivy derived from the Latin, "hedra." It didn't take too long before the real character of this ivy emerged and became known as "yiedra maligna," (evil ivy).

One explanation for the general ignorance regarding Western Poison Oak in the past is that several centuries ago the plant was far less common than it is today. Like its eastern counterparts, the poison ivies, this species is a camp follower and thrives in areas disturbed and disrupted by humans and natural catastrophies. Considering the devastation wrought by frequent earthquakes and forest fires as well as the Gold Rush of 1848 and the population explosion, California is an ideal home for peripatetic Poison Oak.

Poison Oak—western style

The life style of Western Poison Oak is as varied as that of its eastern relative, Climbing Poison Ivy. Not only is *T. diversilobum* California's most prevalent woody shrub but as William Gillis (1933-1979) in his authoritative study, notes, the plant shows the "broadest ecological amplitude in the west." Deserts, dense forests, and altitudes above 4,000 feet are the only restraints to the growth of this species.

Most often Western Poison Oak is an erect shrub, 3 to 5 feet tall with many thin branches, flourishing in disturbed areas, on roadsides, and in uncultivated and abandoned fields. The many abandoned gold and silver mine sites and ghost towns in California are now occupied by prospering Poison Oak populations.

This unwelcome weed grows as spreading thickets in open fields shunned by cattle and ranchers, reducing available grazing acreage. Upright structures (trees, poles, fences, canyon walls, and cliff sides) bring out the inborn climbing impulse of the species and aerial roots that go with it, behavior identical with that of *Toxicodendron radicans.*

The edges of woodlands and clearings are another favored playground and almost any tree becomes a ladder on which it may climb 30 or more feet. The notable exception is Redwood forests, where Poison Oak is relatively rare. Redwoods, noted for longevity and resistance to intruders, discourage climbers; their thick foliage screens light and minimizes the growth of underbrush.

On the other hand, parks, camping and picnic grounds, places frequented by people, hold a special attraction for Western Poison Oak.

Leaf diversity—*diversilobum*

The leaves of Western Poison Oak are extremely variable in shape, a trait inscribed in its scientific epithet *diversilobum.* The trifoliate leaves of this dangerous denizen of the west may be deeply, shallowly, symmetrically, or asymmetrically lobed, resembling those of the White Oak; but some leaflets are lobeless with even edges. The surface may be flat but more often curled or crumpled.

In open fields, specimens tend to have dull, dark green leathery leaflets; in moist shady settings they are light green, thin, and delicate.

Western Poison Oak *(Toxicodendron diversilobum)* shown here climbing a tree trunk. The trifoliate leaves are alternate, the leaflets are largely lobeless, a not too common variant for this species. (E.F.)

The color of the leaflets also varies. The young emergent spring leaves are generally pale green, occasionally red. By summer, they turn yellow-green and shades of red. Fall colors range from spectacular scarlet to ravishing red-purple. They stand out against the parched semidesert western background and add contrast to the otherwise dull landscape. At the same time, the red leaves are a signal: stop, look, and leave.

Trifoliate leaves are usually but not always present. Populations with additional leaflets are not uncommon; 5-leaflet forms, quinquefolia, occur with some regularity and specimens with as many as 17 leaflets have been seen and reported.

Keeping in mind its diversity, Western Poison Oak is distinguishable from other trifoliate *Toxicodendron* species primarily by its west coast habitat. In other respects—flowers, fruits, woody wandering stolons, climbing hairy stems, naked fuzzy buds, and an oily sap that leaves a black mark and a rash—*T. diversilobum* is a true *Toxicodendron*.

5

SUMACS: HARMFUL AND HARMLESS

THE FIFTH MEMBER of the all-American *Toxicodendron* team is Poison Sumac, *T. vernix,* least common and least known of the toxic quintet. Its closest relatives are the Oriental Lacquer and Wax trees, native to eastern Asia, half way around the world. Despite distances, the American Poison Sumac, the Oriental Lacquer Tree, and Wax Tree are so much alike in general appearance and toxicity that there was considerable taxonomic confusion and disagreement among early botanists in distinguishing among them.

The real poison tree—our native Poison Sumac

Poison Sumac is known by a host of descriptive folknames such as Poison Wood, Poison Tree, Poison Weed, Poison Dogwood, Poison Elder, Poison Ash, Swamp Sumac, Varnish Sumac, Varnish Tree, and Thunderwood. These common names reveal some popular conceptions and misconceptions about this species. Poison Sumac is no more related to the dogwoods than to elders or ashes. The names Varnish Sumac and Varnish Tree are echoes of the past when the American Poison Sumac and the Oriental Varnish Tree were thought to be members of the same species. Poison Wood, Poison Tree, and Poison Weed are the earliest titles given to the species by explorers, colonists, and botanists who had personal contact with this plant as they sloshed their way through the swamps and bogs of the east coast of North America. Regardless of common names, to some botanists and all its victims, Poison Sumac is our most poisonous plant species.

Vernix: an erroneous epithet

At present, Poison Sumac carries the binomial *Toxicodendron vernix.* However, for over two centuries, it was known as

Rhus vernix by courtesy of Linnaeus. The epithet "vernix" means varnish or lacquer, a misnomer but acceptable at the time of the christening since, as previously mentioned, the American and Oriental Sumacs were thought to be members of the same species. Regardless of accuracy, this Linnaean epithet has priority over other names since it was validly published before all other proposed epithets according to the International Code of Botanical Nomenclature.

Profile of Poison Sumac

Unlike its trifoliate colleagues, Poison Sumac prefers a moist menage, in or near woody, boggy, and swampy areas of the Eastern United States and Canada from Quebec to Florida and westward along the Gulf Coast into eastern Texas. Some specimens find their way out of the swamps but do not grow as tall as their wetland brothers and sisters.

Few people venture into these swampy habitats and fewer are able to recognize this toxic tree either in a dry or wet setting. Being the least known, it is the most dangerous of the poisonous sumacs. In this case, "What you don't know, can hurt you."

Strictly speaking, only Poison Sumac should be titled *Toxicodendron,* Poison Tree, since it is the only native member of the genus that is truly a tree, not a creeper, a vine, or a subshrub. Mature Poison Sumac trees range in height from 6 to 20 feet. Their alternate leaves are pinnately compound with anywhere from 7 to 13 lobeless, toothless leaflets arranged in a featherlike fashion with the odd leaflet at the free end. Furthermore, it is not too difficult to understand how the feathered compound leaves of Poison Sumac are confused with the leaves of ash, elder, walnut, and the harmless sumacs that frequently grow nearby.

Except for its dendritic demeanor (treelike form) and feathered foliage, *T. vernix* is a tried and true *Toxicodendron*. In the spring the young leaves are bright orange; later they turn dark green and in the fall, brilliant shades of yellow, orange, red, and

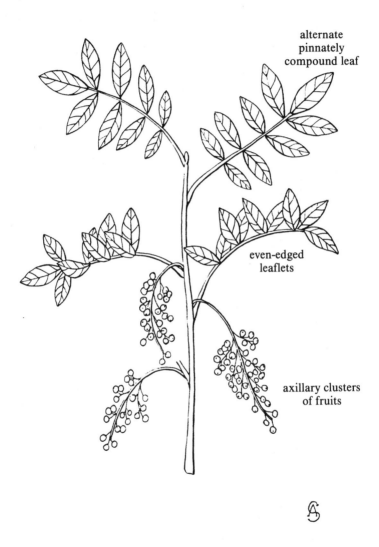

alternate
pinnately
compound leaf

even-edged
leaflets

axillary clusters
of fruits

Poison Sumac *(Toxicodendron vernix)* is largely an eastern wetland tree. The branch seen supports four alternate, pinnately compound leaves. The leaflets are lobeless and even edged. Three Poison Ivy/Poison Oak-like clusters of fruits hang from the leaf axil.

russet, hardly distinguishable from the equally colorful leaves of nonpoisonous sumacs. To the compulsive collector of autumnal leaves, Poison Sumac foliage is irresistible. Some foragers who gather beautiful bouquets of fall foliage may enjoy the fruits of their labors briefly but do not understand why they are afflicted with a severe rash a day or two later.

As is customary among Toxicodendrons, axillary clusters of tiny sweet-smelling male and female flowers grow on separate trees that are insect pollinated and give rise to long, loose bunches of whitish drupes each containing a single seed.

The Oriental Lacquer Tree

This ancient Asiatic tree, a close relative of Poison Sumac, is also known as Varnish Tree, Varnish Lacquer Tree, Chinese Lacquer Tree, Japanese Lacquer Tree, and by various combinations of these appellations. In China, it is "che shu" and in Japan "tsuta urushi." Currently it carries the binomial *Toxicodendron vernicifluum,* a name adopted about 50 years ago that is slowly gaining acceptance in botanical circles.

Until the beginning of the 18th century, the Lacquer Tree was unknown outside the Orient. During the latter part of the 17th century, European botanists first gained entrance to the Far East and began to explore and collect flora never seen before. Among these early plant hunters was Engelbert Kaempfert (1651-1716), a German physician who served as ships' doctor for the Dutch East India Company. For almost a decade, he studied and collected Javanese and Japanese flora. He returned to Holland and in 1712 published his botanical observations with beautiful floral illustrations, including the Oriental Lacquer Tree, which he called "True Lacquer Tree," and the Wax Tree, "False Lacquer Tree."

As previously noted, the native Poison Sumac and the Oriental Lacquer Tree were considered one and the same species named *Rhus vernix* by Linnaeus. It took a century before the Japanese-American taxonomic tie was broken and the Lacquer

Tree won its independence from Poison Sumac and was dubbed *Rhus vernicifera.* Another century passed before the tree was transferred to the genus *Toxicodendron* and was given its present binomial.

The Lacquer Tree may grow to a height of 80 feet and bears large short-stalked compound leaves consisting of 11 to 15 leaflets with entire edges that are fuzzy underneath. It has unisexual pendulous clusters of yellowish-white flowers that mature into yellowish drupe fruits. By virtue of flowers, fruits, and poisonous sap, *T. vernicifluum* qualifies as a member of the genus.

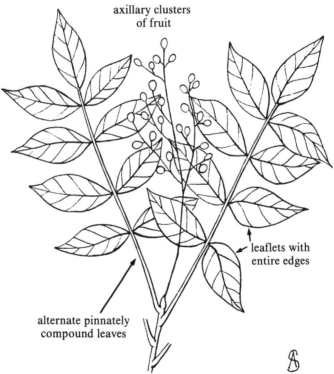

Oriental Lacquer Tree *(Toxicodendron vernicifluum)* is the source of a poisonous sap used for varnishes. A branch illustrated here resembles Poison Sumac with foot-long, alternate, pinnately compound leaves and axillary clusters of whitish drupe fruits. The tree is one of the tallest in the genus.

The tree grows wild in many parts of China and Japan but is cultivated for its sap, a natural varnish, which is of great commercial value. The sap is obtained by slashing and bleeding the tree trunk, a method similar to that used to tap rubber trees; this practice has been going on in China since prehistoric times. The lacquer that oozes out of the wound darkens, thickens, and hardens when exposed to air. It is therefore applied before it hardens and takes on a high sheen. It is used to varnish toys, dishes, clocks, lampshades, wall paper, furniture, and wooden shoes, giving them a hard, shiny finish for which lacquerwear is world famous.

The sap of the Lacquer Tree is also the source of the infamous *Toxicodendron* torment, a dermatitis that is an occupational disease of farmers and factory workers handling this varnish. It contains the same rash-inducing substances present in other members of the genus.

The toxicity of the sap is unbelieveably longlived. A tale is told about the excavation of a thousand-year-old tomb of a Chinese nobleman that contained lacquered furniture. Some of the workers handling these ancient treasures developed classical cases of dermatitis similar to the rash from fresh Lacquer Tree, Poison Ivy, or Poison Oak sap.

A somewhat similar situation was reported involving American GIs stationed in post-World War II Japan who patronized a bar with freshly lacquered furniture and toilet seats. Several were surprised when a Poison Ivy-like rash blossomed on various parts of their anatomy.

The Oriental Wax Tree

The Wax Tree, also known as the Red Lac Tree, is another ancient plant native to China and Japan, where it has been cultivated for centuries. Originally, it was part of the Sino-American Poison Sumac potpouri. However, in 1771 Linnaeus came to the rescue and gave it species status with its own *Rhus* epithet "succedanea" which means "substitute." About a century ago, it was joined to the *Toxicodendron* crowd with the binomial *T. succedaneum;* the Linnaean epithet remained.

Near the end of the branches of this smooth, hairless, medium-sized tree, are leaves that turn bright red before being shed. The alternate, compound leaves, unisexual flowers, and drupe fruits closely resemble those of its cousin, the Lacquer Tree.

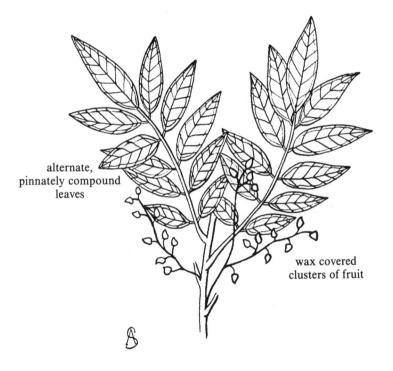

alternate, pinnately compound leaves

wax covered clusters of fruit

Oriental Wax Tree *(Toxicodendron succedaneum)* a close relative of the Oriental Lacquer Tree, is medium-sized. The branch shows alternate, pinnately compound leaves bearing leaflets with even edges and axillary clusters of wax-covered drupe fruits. The sap causes dermatitis in some people.

The tree is valued more for the wax that covers the fruit than for its sap, which yields a poor quality of lacquer but a good case of dermatitis. The wax, called sumac wax or Japanese tallow, is used as a substitute for beeswax, also in varnishes, ointments, and floor wax. Oils extracted from the seeds serve as an illuminant.

Safe Sumacs: *Rhus*

In the northeastern United States and Canada there are several nonpoisonous sumacs that are easily and frequently mistaken for Poison Sumac. Three of the most common species are shrubs with pinnately compound leaves that resemble the foliage of their caustic cousin. They are Smooth Sumac, *Rhus glabra;* Staghorn Sumac, *R. typhina;* and Winged or Dwarf Sumac, *R. copallina.* This nontoxic trio, which is far more common than Poison Sumac, grows along roadsides, dry woods and clearings in sprawling communities. Unfortunately, they cross paths with Poison Sumac and the common grounds on which they meet is where the danger lurks.

The easiest way to tell the "safe" from the "sinister" sumacs is by their fruits, which appear in late summer and fall. The "safe" sumacs wear red hats, conspicuous clusters of reddish fruits at the ends of upturned branches, hard to miss. The "sinister" sumacs bear loose bunches of hanging white to gray fruits along the stems.

Leaf characteristics are also helpful in distinguishing between friend and foe. The edges of the leaflets of both Smooth and Staghorn Sumac are saw-toothed (serrate); those of Winged Sumac are even-edged (entire). In Winged Sumac, the rachis (the part of the leaf stem with leaflets) is flattened or winged, the source of its name. Poison Sumac leaflets are entire and the rachis is round, not winged.

The stems and branches of Staghorn Sumac are covered by a thick layer of short brown hairs that resembles the velvet on the antlers of a male deer, the stag, which accounts for its folk name. It is also called Velvet Sumac for obvious reasons. Smooth Sumac looks very much like Staghorn but lacks the downy decorations; the branches are smooth and shiny, hence its common appellation.

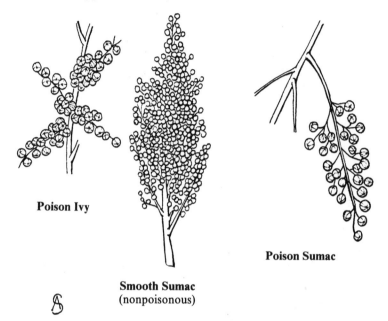

Poison Ivy

Poison Sumac

Smooth Sumac
(nonpoisonous)

Fruits of Poison Ivy, Smooth Sumac, and Poison Sumac. The drawings depict the fruits of Poison Ivy and Poison Sumac in axillary pendulous clusters and those of Smooth Sumac in dense, upright, terminal bunches, typical of nonpoisonous sumacs. Moreover, the fruits of poisonous sumacs *(Toxicodendron)* are whitish, whereas the fruits of nonpoisonous sumacs *(Rhus)* are reddish.

The fourth and rarest member of the local safe sumacs is *Rhus aromatica,* Aromatic or Fragrant, Lemon, or Polecat Sumac, the latter name used by those who find its effluvium skunklike. The confusing feature of this species is its trifoliate leaves, which has caused both amateur and professional botanists to mistake it for a trifoliate in the genus *Toxicodendron.*

There are several other helpful distinguishing characteristics. Aromatic Sumac is a short shrub which bears spikelike clusters of yellow flowers about the time the leaves appear. When crushed the leaves emit a very distinct aroma which some people find pleasant and others offensive. In summer, it flashes clusters of fuzzy, upright red fruits, the safe sumac signal.

This highly variable species nestles in rocky soil, hills, woods, and sand dunes. Its range extends from Quebec to Florida, Texas, and other central and western states.

When all is said and done, "by their fruits ye shall know them," that is, the safe sumacs by upright terminal clusters of red fruits and the troublesome Toxicodendrons by axillary drooping bunches of whitish drupes.

Aromatic Sumac *(Rhus aromatica)* a nonpoisonous shrub with trifoliate leaves, resembling those of Poison Ivy and Poison Oak. The leaves are covered with dense hairs, fragrant when crushed, and the fruit clusters are upright and red. (E.F.)

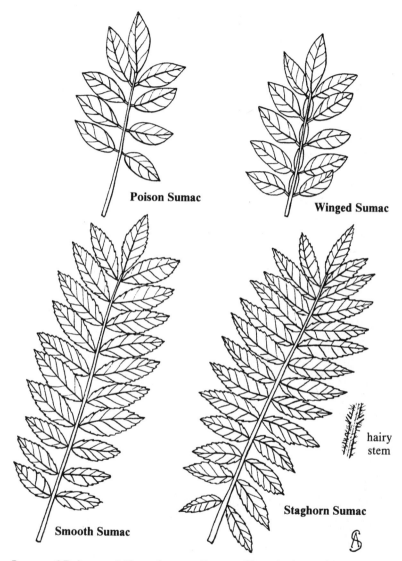

Poison Sumac

Winged Sumac

Smooth Sumac

Staghorn Sumac

hairy stem

Leaves of Poison and Nonpoisonous Sumacs. Note the leaves illustrated are all pinnately compound and may lead to confusion between poisonous and nonpoisonous sumacs. However, the leaflet edges of Smooth and Staghorn Sumacs are saw-toothed (serrate); those of Winged and Poison Sumac are entire. The rachis of Winged Sumac is flattened or winged and that of Poison Sumac is round. Characteristically, stems and branches of Staghorn Sumac are covered with a thick layer of brownish hairs.

6

RELATIVES OF THE TOXICODENDRONS

THE Rhuses and Toxicodendrons so far discussed are a very small sample of the Cashew family, which has a worldwide membership of over 600 species. The family known botanically as the Anacardiaceae or anacardiums derives its name from the heart-shaped (cardium) fruit found in some species. Most are tropical or subtropical, unfamiliar to many Americans, except for the mango, cashew, and pistachio, which are known by their fruits. Not all are poisonous but many carry the family trademark: a 5-parted flower with a 3-parted style and a single-celled ovary forming a drupe.

The Brazilian Pepper Tree—undesirable alien

The Brazilian Pepper Tree, alias Florida Holly, alias Christmas Berry, is not only an undesirable alien but is also clearly misnamed; the fruit is neither a pepper nor a berry but a single-seeded drupe, which is common to the anacardiums.

Its current binomial is *Schinus terebinthifolius;* the first or genus name is pronounced "shyness" hardly descriptive of its aggressive behavior. The name is also pronounced "skyness" a more accurate representation of its tall stature. The second word or epithet (tere-binth-i-fo'-lius), a real tongue twister, relates to the pungent terpentine-like aroma of the leaves.

The Brazilian Pepper Tree has alternate, pinnately compound, evergreen leaves each with 3 to 7 leaflets. Its multiple woody stem may grow to a height of 40 feet forming a fairly impenetrable thicket. In *Toxicodendron* tradition, clusters of tiny sweet-smelling, insect-pollinated male and female flowers grow on separate trees. The single-seeded fruits are juicy, aromatic, and pea-size. They turn orange-red in December and are therefore called Christmas berries. The seeds have a peppery taste; hence the name Pepper Tree. A variety of birds and small mammals feed on the colorful seeds, which are also collected as Christmas ornaments.

clusters of
red juicy fruits

Brazilian Pepper Tree *(Schinus terebinthifolius).* Seen here is a branch with axillary clusters of red, juicy fruits; the leaves are pinnately compound with 5 to 7 entire, evergreen leaflets. The tree is poisonous, weedy, and grows in wetlands of southern Florida.

As its common name indicates, *Schinus* is native to South America. It migrated north through Central America and "stole" across the border into Arizona, southern California, and southern Florida about the middle of the 1900s. However, toward the end of the 19th century, this handsome shrubby tree was introduced in southern Florida as an ornamental plant by the United States Department of Agriculture. And until the 1950s, *Schinus* was a well-behaved shrub that "knew" its place. Subsequently, for reasons best known to itself, *Schinus* lost its shyness and went on a botanical "bender," aggressively taking over areas severely disturbed by fires, hurricanes, and developers. It invaded roadsides, power line rights-of-ways, canals, river banks, and especially, abandoned farms and fields. The weed tree has entered Everglades National Park, where it threatens to displace unique swamp flora, a matter of great concern to conservationists. It is also a serious pest in other southern parts of the state. *Schinus* proliferates like a weed, following the growth pattern of its botanical cousins, the poison ivies and poison oaks.

This ubiquitous shrub is also a menace to public health. It is saturated with a highly volatile toxic resin, most abundant when *Schinus* is in flower. The peak of flowering in southern Florida comes in the fall. However, there is no month in which specimens in bloom cannot be found. Contact with the resin either by touch or by inhaling the fragrance of the flowers or leaves, can bring on an itching dermatitis, facial swelling, and eye inflammation. The peppery taste conceals the toxicity of the seeds which in the past were used, by well-intentioned but misinformed chefs, as a condiment in gourmet restaurants under the name of pink peppercorns. No doubt, complaints by diners removed it from the menu. The poisoning principle, present in all parts of the plant, is chemically similar to that permeating the genus *Toxicodendron*.

To protect the local native flora and Floridians against *Schinus*, Dade County passed an ordinance forbidding its importation, cultivation, and transportation (a bit late but better than never). Natives and visitors should get to know *Schinus* on sight, admire it but avoid any contaminating contact with this beautiful but baneful weedy shrub.

The Poison Tree

The Poison Tree, *Metopium toxiferum,* carries a string of folk names some of which confirm its toxic nature such as: Poisonwood, Burn Wood, Doctor Gum, Coral Sumac, and Mountain Manchineel. It populates the Caribbean Islands, Central America, and the east coast of southern Florida, where it flourishes in hammocks, sand dunes, and pine forests. Locally, it is known as the Florida Poison Tree.

Poison Tree *(Metopium toxiferum).* The branch illustrated has alternate, compound leaves with 5 leaflets that are entire and evergreen; the half-inch fruits are shiny and yellowish-orange. This tree, all parts of which are poisonous, is native to the southeast coast of Florida.

The leaves are pinnately compound with 3 to 7 broad, oval, glossy, even-edged, evergreen leaflets. The flowers and fruits are typical of the family: small 5-parted, yellow-green male and female flowers on separate trees. Pendulous, colorful clusters of yellow to orange fruits adorn the tree. Each fruit contains a single brown seed about a quarter of an inch in length.

Damaged bark and foliage exude a sticky, oily toxic sap that thickens and darkens when exposed to air, leaving black spots and smudges behind. All parts of the tree contain this venom which is capable of inflicting a poison ivy-like rash on susceptible unfortunates. If you react to *Toxicodendron* juice, you are a most likely candidate for damage from the sap of the Poison Tree, which is similar in effect to that of Poison Ivy but more powerful and produces a very severe rash.

Natives in the Caribbean Islands disregard its poisonous properties and use the milk of the tree to treat an aching tooth or to induce abortions.

Historically, Poison Tree made the Linnaean list as *Rhus Metopium* L.

India Ink Tree: Bhilawa

This tree, another member of the Cashew family, is native to India and the Far East, where it is known as the Dhobi Nut Tree or Marking Nut Tree. The binomial bestowed upon it by Linnaeus' son Carl (1741-1783) two centuries ago is *Semecarpus anacardium* L.f. (*seme,* mark; *karpos,* fruit). The entire tree is saturated with a toxic sap that resembles the poisonous *Toxicodendron* rash-inducing resin.

The leaves are alternate, simple, a foot or more long; the flowers are typical of the family; and the fruit is a 1-inch shiny, black, compressed structure set in a fleshy, orange-colored, disc-shaped receptacle. The sap of the young fruit hardens into a black resin and, when mixed with lime water, is used as an ink or dye.

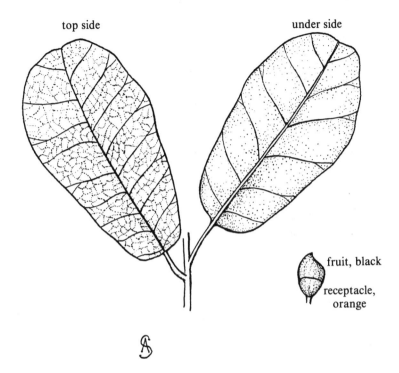

top side   under side

fruit, black

receptacle,
orange

India Ink Tree *(Semecarpus anacardium)*. The leaves of this Asiatic tree are simple, alternate, and average about one foot in length. The fruit is a black, shiny drupe seated in a fleshy orange receptacle (fruit stalk). All parts of the tree are poisonous.

The fruit is called dhobi nut; dhobi is the Indian name for laundrymen who use the black ink to mark laundry. The markings are indelible and become darker with successive washings. Similarly, American Indians and early settlers in the New World used the juice of local Toxicodendrons as a dye and for marking clothes.

During World War II, some American servicemen stationed in India were plagued with a poison ivy-like rash on the neck, wrist, waist, and more intimate parts of the body. The source of their troubles was traced to the dhobi markings.

The Mango Tree

This member of the Cashew family, best known for its fruit, the mango, is at home in India, where it has been cultivated for more than 4,000 years. The tree is sacred to Buddhists and Hindus, who revere it as a symbol of health, wealth, and happiness. About one third of the world's mangoes is grown in India where it is called "Fruit of Heaven." Over a thousand varieties have been developed and introduced into tropical and subtropical regions of the world including Mexico, Haiti, Central America, and southern Florida, where some have escaped and are growing wild.

The scientific name of this tree is *Mangifera indica* L. "mango-bearing plant of India," a Linnean binomial still in use. The English name is derived from the Portugese word "manga," which in turn is a corruption of "mankai," from Tamil, the language spoken by the people of southern India. Indian folklore relates the story of Buddha, who was presented with a mango grove by his disciples. There, in the shade, he would find repose and teach his followers how to escape to Nirvana.

The fame of the delicious mango fruit overshadows its infamy as a source of dermatitis. The toxin is a resinous sap called cardol that is chemically similar to the poisonous substances found in *Toxicodendron* and with the same dermatitic effect on sensitive individuals. Cardol is present in all parts of the plant, including the floral scent and the skin of the fruit, but not the edible juicy pulp.

The Mango Tree is tall, dark green, and handsome, reaching a height of 75 feet or more. The broad crown of dense foliage consists of simple, alternate, leathery, evergreen, shiny, lance-shaped leaves, often with wavy edges; when bruised, the leaves give off a sweet aroma. Myriads of minute yellow or red male and bisexual fragrant flowers occur in long-branched, hanging clusters. The floral structure is typical of the family. The fruits, which range in size from apples to cantaloups, have a thin skin that turns red tinged with yellow or green, depending upon the variety. The skin

covers the edible sweet orange or yellow colored pulp surrounding a large flat stone, inside of which is a single seed.
Some varieties have a turpentine odor and flavor, a gourmet's
delight or disappointment.

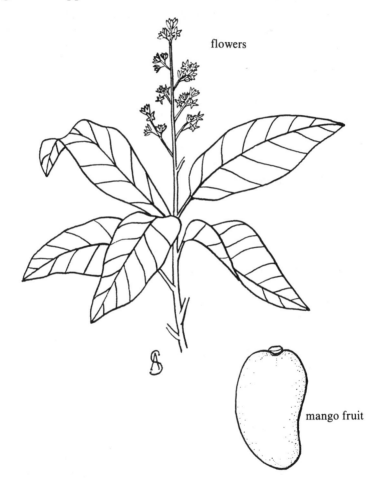

flowers

mango fruit

Mango Tree *(Mangifera indica)*. The branch shown bears five one-foot
long simple, entire, evergreen, alternate leaves and a stalk of fragrant red or
yellow flowers. The fruit, on the average, is grapefruit-size, egg-shaped with
a red skin tinged with green or yellow. The sweet, orange-colored pulp is
nonpoisonous whereas all other parts of the tree are toxic. The tree, native
to India, has been introduced and cultivated in tropical and subtropical
countries worldwide, including southern Florida.

For most people, the mango is a gastronomic treat—more so when they learn to manage the gushy pulp that tends to cling to the large slippery seed. However, some are not so fortunate; they come away from a mango meal with a mango mouth, an oral poison ivy-like rash, from the poisonous peel. Damaged mango foliage permits cardol to drip on the fruit rind, further contaminating it. Also, the floral scent is capable of causing facial rashes and eye irritations.

If you are "mad" for mangoes, wash them thoroughly and peel before sticking your face, hands, and mouth on them. Do not smell the flowers, or you will discover that messing with mangoes may leave you with a rash reminder.

Mangos also have a place in folk medicine. In India and Panama, the leaves and twigs are used to treat bronchitis, catarrh, internal bleeding, and as a mouthwash and gargle. The bark relieves toothaches and the skin of the fruit stops uterine bleeding.

The Cashew Tree

The Cashew Tree, although famous for its fruit, the cashew nut, is less well known for its "oil of dermatitis," a potent poison found in the wall of the nut. A native of northeastern Brazil and the lower Amazon, it has been introduced and flourishes as a valuable cash crop in tropical America from Mexico to Peru, the West Indies, the south coast of Florida, and around the world in Madagascar, India, and Malaysia.

Its English name comes from "caju" the Portugese term used by the early settlers in Brazil; "caju" is a corruption of "acaju," derived from the local Brazilian Indian language.

The tree can grow to a height of 30 feet with a spreading crown. The leaves are simple, entire, dull blue-green, leathery, evergreen, alternate, and about 6 inches long. Small fragrant, 5-parted, yellow-green male and bisexual flowers develop in terminal clusters on the same tree.

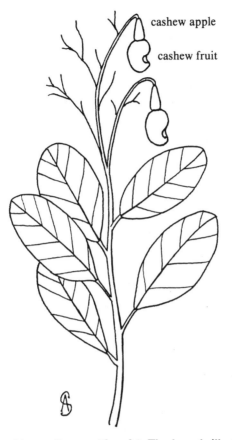

cashew apple

cashew fruit

Cashew Tree *(Anacardium occidentale)*. The branch illustrated, bears 5 simple, oval, entire, evergreen leaves that are alternately positioned. The fruit, a kidney-shaped drupe, hangs from the free end of a red or yellow pear-shaped, pulpy, eatible fruit stalk, the cashew apple. The poisonous chemicals, in the wall of the cashew nut, are destroyed by roasting. The tree is native to northeastern Brazil but is cultivated in many other tropical countries around the world.

The fruit is most unusual in its location; it is borne at the end of a pulpy, edible, pear-shaped, hanging fruit stalk called a "cashew apple." The fruit itself is a 1-inch hanging drupe that looks like a kidney bean or a miniature boxing glove. Perhaps it was the shape of the cashew apple or the fruit that inspired

Linnaeus to name the tree *Anacardium occidentale*, (*anacardium*, heart-shaped; *occidentale*, Western World).

The cashew nut is enclosed in a smooth, hard, green-colored shell that is brown or grey when ripe. The fruit is cracked to free the much sought-after kernel while the highly toxic oil, an important commercial by-product, is extracted from the cashew nut wall.

The highly nutritious nut is made edible by roasting, which destroys the toxic oil. The cashew nut wall extract contains anacardic acid, cardinol, and cardol, the latter with the same chemical structure and rash-provoking properties as the toxins in *T. radicans*. Factory workers who handle cashew nut shells or are exposed to the fumes of the roasting process, are frequent victims of eye, skin, and lung irritations. Smoke particles from burning cashew wood carry droplets of caustic cardol causing reactions similar to burning Poison Ivy or its ilk.

Cashew nut oil has an amazing variety of commercial and medical applications, some of questionable value. It is used as an insecticide for termite-proofing lumber; to make plastics, varnish, lubricants, and as an indelible ink to mark cotton and linen since it turns black when exposed to air. Anacardic acid kills malaria-carrying mosquitoes and roundworms.

In folk medicine, cashew has been used in the treatment of scurvy; to remove corns, warts, and freckles; to treat burns, psoriasis, and ringworm; as a gargle for sore throats; to heal cracks on the soles of feet; to cure sore gums and toothaches; and as a remedy for snakebites. In East India and Tanzania, the oil is used for tattooing. Similarly, West Coast American Indians used Poison Oak sap for the same purpose. The natives of the West Indies apply cashew oil cosmetically, to get a new look and complexion. The oil produces a severe skin rash with blistering, festering, and exfoliation of the facial skin. A "new" face emerges but what a price for vanity.

The Pistachio Tree

The fame and fortune of the Pistachio Tree rests on its fruit, the pistachio nut. Evidence of its existence goes back 9,000 years based on radioactive carbon dating of material excavated in Jordan. The tree was well known to the inhabitants of Eastern Asia and Asia Minor for millenia and was introduced in the Mediterranean countries about the dawn of the Christian era. On the Linnaean roster, Pistachio is listed as *Pistacia vera*, the genuine Pistachio.

Pistachio nuts are mentioned in the *Bible*. In the *Book of Genesis,* Jacob sends his sons to Egypt to buy corn since "the famine was sore in the land." He tells them:

". . . take of the choice of foods of the land in your vessel and carry them down to the man [Joseph, Grand Visier, whom the brothers sold into Egyptian slavery] a present, a little balm, and a little honey, spicery, and ladanum, nuts [pistachios], and honey, . . ."

Another famous biblical personality, the Queen of Sheba, was allegedly a pistachio nut addict. She had a monopoly on the supply of Assyrian pistachios, which she kept for herself and court favorites.

Pistachios are widely cultivated in the dry, warm, and temperate climate of Afghanistan, Greece, Turkey, Syria, and especially Iran which is a major pistachio exporter. Within the last two decades, extensive areas in the Sacramento and San Joaquin Valleys of California have been given over to growing the nut.

The Pistachio Tree grows to a height of about 30 feet and bears pinnately compound deciduous leaves that are deciduous (shed annually), with 3 to 5 entire leaflets. Tiny greenish-brown unisexual flowers lacking petals, nectar, and aroma grow on separate trees and are wind pollinated. A male Pistachio serves a bevy of about a dozen female trees. After pollination and fertilization, the pistillate flowers develop grapelike clusters of fruits with reddish outer hulls that cover light tan-colored shells which in turn enclose green to yellow edible kernels (seeds). The

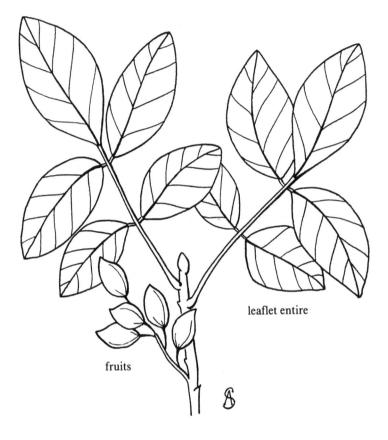

leaflet entire

fruits

Pistachio Tree *(Pistachia vera)* seen here is a branch with two alternate, compound leaves, each with five entire leaflets. Also shown is a small cluster of fruits, five pistachio nuts. Inside the shell is a green to yellow edible kernel. Pistachios are cultivated in warm, dry climates of eastern Asia and California.

nuts, similar in size and shape to olives, are salted and/or roasted for flavor. They are marketed either naturally colored (light tan), or artificially dyed (bright red).

Domestic, mechanized harvesting techniques produce naturally colored nuts, free of blemishes. Imported pistachios are mostly hand processed, the old fashioned way that leaves the nuts with unsightly markings; to conceal these blemishes, they are dyed red. Some red-dyed pistachios are also produced domestically, using nontoxic dyes approved by the Food and Drug Administration.

Although *Pistachio vera* is a member of the Cashew family, it has no black marks against it and the nuts are perfectly safe to eat and enjoy.

The American Smoke Tree

Lest you are left with the impression that all American anacardiums, except the safe sumacs, are venomous, meet the American Smoke Tree, also known as Chittam-Wood. Currently, its binomial is *Cotinus obovatum* formerly known as *Rhus cotinoides* and classified as a sumac species.

Our native Smoke Tree is comparatively rare, restricted to the rocky hills and bluffs of a few southern states. It is a short tree or shrub with strong-smelling yellow wood of no commercial value. The leaves are alternate, simple, entire, thin in texture, and oval-to-egg shaped; they turn brilliant orange to red before being shed in the fall.

Cotinus flowers and fruits meet the requirements of a recognized anacardium: 5-parted yellow to green flowers in clusters; male flowers with 5 stamens and female flowers with a single 3-parted pistil usually on separate trees and a single seeded kidney-shaped drupe. However, the fruits of *Cotinus* are very tiny and few in number.

The common name, Smoke Tree, aptly describes the unforgetable appearance of the tree in summer. The large terminal clusters of flowers contain mostly sterile blossoms, the stalks of which elongate and grow mostly white fluffy hairs. This creates the illusion of a tree covered with wispy puffs of smoke, a beautiful sight to behold and the pride of many horticulturists.

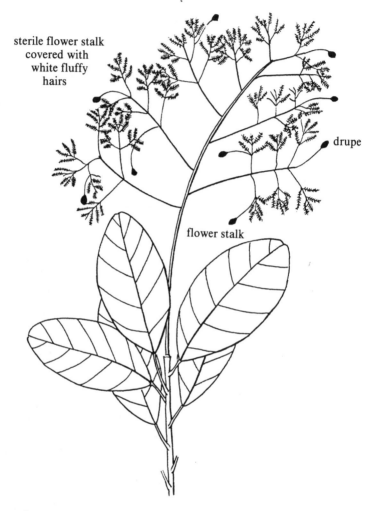

sterile flower stalk covered with white fluffy hairs

drupe

flower stalk

American Smoke Tree *(Cotinus obovatum)* the branch illustrated holds 5 oval-shaped, entire, alternate leaves and a foot-long terminal flowering stem. A few very tiny kidney-shaped drupes are seen on the tips of threadlike flower stalks. Most are the stalks of sterile flowers covered with white fluffy hairs that create the typical smoke effect. The tree is rare and limited to the rocky hills in a few southern states.

Equally, if not more spectacular, is the European Smoke Tree, *Cotinus coggygria*, known in the Old World since antiquity and cultivated in the United States as an ornamental. The leaves and fruits of the European species are smaller than those of its American cousin. However, the flowers are quite variable; they are mostly bisexual but may also be unisexual with male and female flowers on separate trees or on different parts of the same tree. The smoke puffs are larger and more showy and never fail to attract attention as a spectacular showpiece in any garden. Regardless of its beauty, be cautious since there are reports that the European species may cause a skin rash.

European Smoke Tree *(Cotinus coggygria)* is a nonpoisonous ornamental shrub or small tree that closely resembles its American counterpart. Note the egg-shaped simple leaves and the clusters of tiny whitish-green flowers that appear in the summer. (E.F.)

7

TALES OF *TOXICODENDRON* TOXINS
FACT AND FICTION

THE *Toxicodendron*-dermatitis connection was probably made when people first come in close contact with these poisonous plants. The earliest records of this relationship go back to the fifth century writings of Chinese scholars, who describe dermatitis as an occupational disease among farmers and factory workers handling the Oriental Lacquer tree and its products.

However, it was not until a thousand years later that Europeans became aware of the existence of a North American *Toxicodendron* species. Captain John Smith (1580-1631), English explorer, adventurer, romantic, and founder of the Jamestown colony in Virginia, is credited with being the first European to describe Poison Ivy and the skin rash it causes. In a letter to England in 1609, he remarks:

"The poisonous weed, being in shape, but very little different, from our English Yvie; but being touched causeth reddness, itchinge and lastly blysters, the which howsoever after a while they pass away of themselves with out further harme . . .'

Poison Ivy, the name Smith gave to this plant, is again described in his book *The General Histories of Virginia, New England and the Summer Isles,* published in 1624:

"... yet for the time they [Poison Ivy] are somewhat painfull and in aspect dangerous, it hath gotten itself an ill name although questionless of no ill nature."

The notion that this weed is "of no ill nature" likely was not shared by fellow colonists or local Indians, friend or foe. The

Jamestown colony did not survive but Smith's account of Poison Ivy did and the name he gave it made botanical history.

Venomous Vapors

Early American explorers, colonists, physicians, and botanists were painfully aware of the Toxicodendrons as agents of the "rhus rash" as it was then known. However, they were unaware of all the ways in which this awful affliction was contracted. Until the end of the 19th century, the prevailing belief was that Poison Ivy and Poison Sumac gave off "venomous vapors" that spread the disease.

Paul Dudley (1673-1751), an amateur American botanist, described the "Poyson-Wood Tree," *T. vernix*, as a wetland plant and added:

"... it poysons two ways, either by touching or handling of it, or by the Smell; for the scent of it, when cut down in the Woods, or on the Fire, has poisoned Persons to a very great degree ... this sort of Poyson is never Mortal, and will go off in a few Days of it self, like the Sting of a Bee; but generally the Person applies Plantain Water or Sallet-Oyl and Cream."

Dudley repeated the fashionable fiction of the day, that the venom could be spread by "scent" and prescribed home remedies some of which are still used.

John Clayton (1685-1773), an English barrister and ardent botanist who settled in Virginia and studied its flora, wrote about Climbing Poison Ivy in Latin, which was translated as follows:

"Milky sap falls in drops, when exposed to air quickly turns black. Poison vapors exhaled by all parts of the plant, when bruised give rise to irritating pustules, swellings and pains in the body."

The "poison vapor" idea is repeated by Clayton which further added credence to this misleading myth.

Another "venomous vapor" proponent was Peter Kalm (1717-1779), one of Linnaeus' prize students who came to the United States and spent two and a half years studying and collecting east coast flora. Based on his observations and first-hand experiences with Poison Sumac as a physician and botanist, he wrote:

"... the nature of some persons will not allow them to approach the place where the tree [Poison Sumac] grows, or to expose themselves to the wind when it carries the effluvia or exhalations of this tree with it ..."

He also encountered Poison Ivy and reported:

"I have seen people who have been much swelled from the noxious exhalations of the latter [Poison Ivy]. ... I likewise know, that of two sisters, the one could manage the tree without being affected by its venom, though the other immediately felt it as soon as the exhalations of the tree came near her, or whenever she came a yard too near the tree, or even when she stood in the way of the wind, which blew directly from this shrub."

The "evil effluvium" theory was also supported by Thomas Horsfield (1773-1859), an American physician who in his M.D. thesis wrote:

"The rash is often produced by the exhalations or effluvium of the plants [Poison Ivy and Poison Sumac]. ... My observation leads me to believe that in very excitable habits it extends from 15 to 20 feet."

Horsfield went one step further by quantifying the range of the evil exhalations and so adding to their credibility.

An eminent physician and professor of Medical Botany at Harvard University, John Bigelow (1787-1879), added his name to the list of Poison Sumac "effluvium" advocates by writing:

"The effluvium of this shrub is a violent poison to certain constitutions, producing in them a distressing cutaneous eruption when it is handled or even approached."

When the great Asa Gray (1810-1888), physician, Professor of Medical Botany at Harvard University, and dean of American botanists, accepted the "evil effluvium" concept, who dared argue against it? He stated that Poison Ivy, which he called *Rhus venenata* rather than by the more popular binomial *Rhus radicans*

"... is the most dangerous species, even the effluvium may affect many people."

He was one of the "many people" affected by the effluvium and in a letter to a friend said that he was:

"... very sensitive to the fresh plant ... the poison is volatile as shown by its affecting people who do not touch it actually."

One can sympathize with Gray's *Toxicodendron* sensitivity but is puzzled by his acceptance of the "evil effluvium" theory in view of his extensive experience as plant collector and author of the first five volumes of *Gray's Manual of Botany*, the botanists' bible to the flowering plants and ferns of Central and Northeastern United States and adjacent Canada.

The *Evil Effluvium* Theory Exposed

The "evil" effluvium myth was badly shaken but not completely toppled just before the end of the 19th century by the discoveries of Franz Pfaff (1860-1926), an American physician. He isolated the venom in Poison Ivy by distillation. Then using himself as a guinea pig, proved that it was the nonvolatile oily residue and not the vapors that contained the poisoning principle. This breakthrough was subsequently substantiated by a host of researchers.

Folklore and superstition die slowly. The "vapor" concept is down but not out, at least in the minds and practices of some hardliners. Indeed, there are those who go further and insist that the mere thought, dream, or sight of Poison Ivy make their skin crawl and break out in a rash.

However, it is more productive to explore the nature of *Toxicodendron* toxins and to investigate suspected and unsuspected sources of the disease than to probe occult and mystical origins of spontaneous and psychogenic dermatitis.

The Urushiols: Oil of Dermatitis

The dermatitic damage, itchy bumps and blisters, suffered by millions of Americans annually is due to the oily resin present in *Toxicodendron* irrespective of species, habitat, age, sex, or country of origin. The culprit is called *urushiol* (oo-roo-she-ol), a term derived from "urushi," the Japanese word for lacquer that originally referred to the oily sap of the Oriental Lacquer Tree, tsuta urushi.

Urushiol is a complex mixture of several catechols, ringed chemical compounds with side chains of 15 or 17 carbons, the proportions of which vary in *Toxicodendron* species. If you are sensitive to one of the Toxicodrendrons, you are probably allergic to all.

The oily resin is carried in special microscopic ducts that flow to all parts of the plant except the anthers, pollen grains, hairs, and wood cells. Normally the urushiols are confined to these internal canals and so render intact plants harmless. Hence, seeing, smelling, standing, walking near, or gently touching a *Toxicodendron* is safe. The trouble begins when plant parts are broken, bruised, or insect-bitten allowing urushiol to escape from the ducts onto the surface of leaves, stems, roots, flowers, or fruits.

When exposed to air, the milky sap, enriched with urushiol, oxidizes and quickly hardens into black, sticky, shiny spots or smears easily mistaken for dirt, decay, or disease. Black spots are a warning sign to stop, look, but not to touch unless you are determined to perform a do-it-yourself test for sensitivity to Toxicodendrons.

On the other hand, the tendency of the urushiols to darken on exposure to air is used in the "Black Spot" test which can assist in identifying poison ivies, oaks, and sumacs as well as other species of *Toxicodendron*. This test is briefly described in the May 1990 issue of *The Executive Health Report* as follows. First, collect a leaf with stem avoiding direct contact with its sap. Second, place the leaf between sheets of white paper and press down until the urushiol-laden sap oozes out. Finally, expose the pressed leaf to the air and note that if the leaf is a species of *Toxicodendron,* the wet spots turn brown within minutes and black in a few hours.

The Long-Lived Urushiols

The urushiols are incredibly potent, stable, long-lived, and also very difficult to remove from animate and inanimate objects. Like most plant oils, urushiols readily adhere to and quickly penetrate the human skin. The oils are so potent that a drop the size of a pinhead is enough to provoke skin rashes in half a hundred persons sensitive to urushiols. In fact, as little as one part in a million is enough to set off a rash.

To avoid or minimize dermatitis, the strategy is to remove the oil as quickly as possible before it is absorbed and initiates a series of internal immune reactions that culminate in a rash.

Time, temperature, and rough treatment seem to have very little effect on urushiol potency. Poison Ivy leaves, *T. radicans*, stored at room temperature for 5 years were almost as toxic as fresh specimens. Branches of the species left out of doors for one year lost little of their venomous vigor. Clothing deliberately contaminated with Poison Ivy sap, a year later produced a ravishing rash. Gloves worn to collect Poison Ivy specimens for class study, stored in a closet for 10 months, then washed with strong soap, dried, and ironed were handed to a volunteer. The following day the student turned up in class with a classical case of Poison Ivy dermatitis.

Add to these experiments, reports of the rhus rash attributed to handling 100 year-old herbarium specimens of *Toxicodendron* and the previously mentioned thousand-year-old lacquered furniture found in the tomb of a Chinese nobleman. As indestructible as the urushiols seem to be, they do their "thing" only on susceptible humans who tamper with Toxicodendrons or their products.

Urushiol Carriers

Although direct contact with urushiols is the usual route by which they reach us, there are some less obvious and unsuspected roads to rhus dermatitis. Practically anything, dead or alive, animate or inanimate, is a potential urushiol carrier (fomite). Clothing, shoes, garden tools, camping equipment, golf clubs, rubbish, and animal pets are recognized fomites but are sometimes overlooked or disregarded as such. Touching or stroking the fur of a cat or dog that has been rolling and romping in Poison Ivy or Poison Oak patches is as good a way of getting the rash as fondling or petting the plant itself. Remember, fomites are a major source of the rash.

Gardeners, when removing Poison Ivy, may take the precaution of wearing gloves, trousers, and long-sleeved shirts and yet be struck by a rash any time of the year even in the dead of winter. The mystery is solved by noting that after the gardening chores are completed, the urushiol spotted gloves and tools are often touched with bare hands.

Poison Ivy and Poison Oak dermatitis occur most frequently among outdoor workers—lumberjacks, park and forest rangers, and forest firefighters because of their high exposure to these plants. The rash is considered an occupational disease in these groups and is reported as the cause of the most frequent workmen's compensation disability in this country, especially in California and the northwest. These areas with extensive growths of Poison Ivy and Poison Oak are constantly plagued by forest fires that occur more often now than in the past and take a greater toll in valuable timber, property, and human health. A goodly number of firefighters involved in combating these conflagrations are compelled to withdraw from the fire lines because of severe cases of dermatitis.

Whether Toxicodendrons are burned as trash or consumed by the flames of forest fires, the smoke and soot carry tiny droplets of urushiol. These poison-bearing particles rain down causing a rash that may cover the victim from head to toe. Inhaling the smoke may lead to lung infections and death. The rule is never to stand on the windward side of burning *Toxicodendron* for it is indeed an ill wind that blows "venomous vapors."

Urushiol carriers *(fomites)*. Garden tools are frequently overlooked as carriers of urushiols after weeding Poison Ivy or its relatives. To decontaminate such tools as well as other fomites, wash, wash, and wash again with cold, running water.

8

TOXICODENDRON DERMATITIS: AN ALLERGIC DISEASE

URUSHIOL-induced dermatitis is an allergic condition similar to hay fever, hives, and asthma. Just as some people are allergic to foods, chemicals, dust, feathers, mold spores, and pollens, others are sensitive to the urushiols.

Allergies are not contagious like measles or mumps. One does not contract dermatitis from somebody who has the rash but gets it from touching urushiols. Half the population in the United States is sensitive and reacts in varying degrees to this allergen. No one is born with *Toxicodendron*-sensitivity but may acquire it after an experience with the plant.

The first exposures to these plants usually take place during childhood. There is no visible rash or any other external sign of such initial encounters. First episodes are periods of *sensitization* in which the body prepares itself against future urushiol attacks. One is unaware of the extremely complex internal processes that may take weeks to complete, but the final effects may persist for years and perhaps a lifetime.

Subsequent exposures trigger the rash. In these instances, urushiols are transferred from the plant or fomite to individuals, where they penetrate and combine with the cells of the skin. This turns on the body's immune system, which destroys the intruding urushiols as well as the infected skin cells, thus producing the well known rash. Since the rash appears a day or two after contact, it is called delayed contact dermatitis.

Urushiol penetration occurs most frequently in the thin-skinned parts of the body: forearm, ankles, face, eyelids, mucous membranes of the nose and mouth, genital areas, as well as the webbing between the fingers and toes. The areas least affected are the thicker parts of the hide: the palms of the hands, the soles of the feet, and the hairy scalp, which present a physical barrier.

The rash progresses in 3 stages: first, the affected area begins to itch and becomes red and swollen, usually a day or two after contact; second, about 2 days later, small blisters appear which begin to merge; in the last stage, a few days later, large blisters burst and "weep" accumulated body fluid (lymph) for about 4 days.

The itching that accompanies the rash brings on an overwhelming, almost uncontrollable urge to scratch out those "damned spots." If you conquer the scratching urge and there are no further complications, the period of healing begins. The inflamed skin "weeps," crusts, scales, sheds, and regenerates. Within two to four weeks, the dermatitic damage is healed over until the next encounter.

Urushiol-induced rashes are self-limiting, non-fatal diseases in which itching is the most annoying symptom and scratching is the least effective and most damaging response.

Sensitivity to the Urushiols

Responses to the urushiols depend primarily on the amount of oil to which an individual is exposed and the degree of sensitivity. The reactions range from total immunity to hypersensitivity so severe that medical intervention and sometimes hospitalization are necessary.

Sensitivity to the urushiol is subject to change without notice and to that extent is unpredictable and baffling. In general, children are more likely to be sensitized and victimized by the urushiols than adults. Youngsters are less familiar with these plants, tend to be less cautious, and are therefore more often exposed to these wayward, wily, weeds. Adults, having had childhood experiences and painful memories, usually are more cautious and make some efforts to keep hands off *Toxicodendron*. Those who never suffered the torturous rash or have long forgotten their childhood bouts, often assume that they are immune, only to discover how painfully wrong they are.

A biology teacher, who should have known better, showed Poison Ivy to his classes and to demonstrate his immunity rubbed his arms, face, and neck with the foliage. As a finale, he chewed a few leaves as he cautioned his students to "Do as I say, not as I do." This went on for several years until one not so nice day, he came down with a rash so severe as to land him in a hospital for several weeks. The moral of the story is "Never take a *Toxicodendron* for granted" and never assume that immunity to the urushiols is forever. It is foolhardy to tempt the fates by tampering with these noxious weeds.

Most people, however, are more fortunate; the older they get, the less sensitive they become to the *Toxicodendron* touch. Nevertheless, there are exceptions and you may be one of them. Eternal vigilance is the price for freedom from the tyranny of *Toxicodendron*.

The Skin Patch Test for Urushiol Sensitivity

Clearly, past history of reactions to urushiols is not necessarily indicative of present status. Doctors William Epstein and Vera Byers, West Coast *Toxicodendron* experts, developed a simple skin test to measure levels of sensitivity to the urushiols, similiar to the patch test for tuberculosis. A small drop of urushiol oil is placed on the forearm of the subject and two days later the site is examined. It will show either no reaction, a red spot, a red spot with swellings, or a red spot with blisters. The population of the United States may be divided into 4 levels of sensitivity to the urushiols as measured by the patch test. Apparently, 15 to 25 percent of the people are not sensitive; they show no reaction to the patch test. Another 25 percent are mildly sensitive; they require more than the urushiol in one leaf to react. Between 25 and 30 percent are moderately sensitive and flare up when exposed to the amount of urushiol in one leaf. The very sensitive individuals, 10 to 20 percent, break out in a severe rash when exposed to the urushiol contained in less than one leaf; they are "exquisitely sensitive."

Urushiol Dermatitis: The Inside Story

When urushiols penetrate the skin for the first time, they combine with cell proteins of the dermis, the inner skin. This urushiol-protein complex is an antigen (immune-process initiator); it activates certain kinds of white blood cells, lymphocytes, causing them to multiply. These lymphocytes are said to be sensitized, that is, programmed to respond to future urushiol invasions. They, or their progeny, may persist in the body for months, years, or a lifetime as memory cells. During this initial phase of the immune process no rash or any other external symptoms are visible.

On subsequent urushiol penetration, programmed lymphocytes "recognize" the intruders and set off a series of immunological reactions that result in an inflammatory rash with its characteristic symptoms. Redness is caused by dilation of blood vessels; swelling, by fluid (lymph) leaking from the blood vessels. Blisters may develop filled with lymph. Several kinds of lymphocytes and macrophages (giant scavenger cells), destroy damaged tissue, and healing begins.

Further investigations are underway to improve our understanding of how immunity is acquired and how active cases of urushiol poisoning can best be treated.

9

PREVENTION AND TREATMENT
OF THE *TOXICODENDRON* TERROR

THE BEST WAY to avoid urushiol poisoning is to keep clear of the Toxicodendrons. This is easier said than done as any victim will attest. As has been repeatedly emphasized, first you must be able to recognize *Toxicodendron* as the "poisoners for all seasons," in their guises and disguises. Then, regardless of age, race, color, or previous condition of "immunity," avoid direct or indirect contact with any or all parts of these plants at all times of the year.

Clothing Coverup

The first line of defense against the *Toxicodendron* terror is clothing. The standard spring-summer fashion of shorts, T-shirts, halters, and open sandals or bare feet is appropriate for the season but dangerously inappropriate for walking, jogging, hiking, picnicking, "bundling" or camping in disturbed areas, the favorite haunts of poison ivies and poison oaks. The less naked skin you show, the fewer places and chances there are for these plants to "bite" and leave their "teeth marks" on you. The recommended dress, especially if you know or suspect that you are *Toxicodendron* vulnerable, is slacks, longsleeved shirts, socks, and closed shoes. However, being under clothes cover does not necessarily give you complete protection. Should the urushiols find their way under sweaty clothing, the body heat promotes the absorption of the offending oil and sweat spreads it. With or without protective clothes covering, in the presence of Toxicodendrons, be cautious and keep cool.

Protective Screens

The second line of defense against the urushiols are barriers that block entrance to the skin by coating it with creams, lotions, gels, salves, or sprays. However, many of these alleged screening substances have been tested and found wanting.

An aerosol spray appropriately called Ivy-Bloc contains a natural organic clay, found as a filler in cosmetics and antiperspirants. When sprayed on clothing, tools, or the skin, it acts as a fairly effective urushiol barrier for a day. The spray absorbs the oily urushiols just as antiperspirants absorb the natural oils and sweat of the skin. Ivy-Bloc binds to the toxic oils, thus preventing them from adhering and penetrating the skin.

Ivy-Bloc has been successfully field tested with U.S. Forest Service workers on the West Coast and seems to have a bright future. However, neither Ivy-Bloc nor the many other available protective screens are panaceas that allow you to throw caution to the wind. The search for a "Complete Ivy-Bloc" goes on.

Immunity : An Unrealized Goal

One of the dreams of medical research is to create a one-shot antiurushiol vaccine that will immunize a person for life, a natural gift enjoyed by only one out of four Americans.

There is an oft repeated story that American Indians acquired immunity to *Toxicodendron* by chewing or eating such foliage. Correspondence and conversation with West Coast Indians and ethnobotanists produced contradictory opinions and conjectures. It is possible that native Indians who seemed to be less susceptible to urushiols than white settlers also had extensive herbal knowledge and experience with *Toxicodendron* and learned to handle plants of this genus safely. Furthermore, there are indications that the *Toxicodendron* population was much smaller in precolonial days than it is today. Modern Indians shun this leaf-chewing practice.

For those fortunate individuals who are not sensitive to Toxicodendrons such foliage may make a palatable meal, but for the rest of the population a Poison Ivy salad could be a "last supper." In any event, sensitive or immune, don't dine on any part of Toxicodendrons no matter how tempting it appears.

Natural and synthetic urushiols are being used experimentally to induce immunity. Antiurushiol medications now available are administered topically, orally, or by injection. The principle is to provoke the immune system to destroy or detoxify urushiols without injuring the skin. Thus far, results have been variable and in some cases the treatment is worse than the disease.

Directory of Dermatitic "Cures"

Despite the fact that untreated urushiol rashes run their course and "after a while, they pass away of themselves with out furthere harme," as observed by Captain John Smith, innumerable folk remedies, patent medicines, and "sure fire" cures ranging from the unbelievable to the impossible, have been used to treat hapless victims.

Folk medicine, most of which is of little or no value and may do more harm than good, includes such concoctions as "charcoal from burned poison sumac mixed with hog's fat" or "sallet-oyl and cream." To these recipes may be added, tongue-in-cheek, in alphabetical order from A to Z, the following: ammonia, baking soda, bleach, buttermilk, castor oil, coffee, corn starch, Epsom salts, gasoline, goat's milk, gunpowder, hair spray, horse urine, iodine, kerosine, lysol, marshmallow, meat tenderizer, nail polish, oatmeal, sodium bicarbonate, strychnine, tobacco, toothpaste, whisky, and last but not least, zirconium, a rare chemical element.

Time and again, claims are made that immunity to urushiols can be acquired by drinking milk from goats that feed on Poison Ivy. Dr. Vera Byers, *Toxicodendron* specialist on the West Coast states:

"This is one folk remedy that probably works although it never has been tested. There's something magic about oral doses of urushiol oil, and goat's milk probably has traces of it. If you drink goat's milk you're probably doing about the same thing we are in our vaccine work."

Please note that drinking goat's milk laced with urushiols to acquire immunity is not endorsed by experts. It is as hazardous as chewing on *Toxicodendron* leaves, a practice ascribed to American Indians.

We now turn to Nature's antidotes, herbs favored by the American Indians and early colonists, and not overlooked by modern herbalists. The most popular antiurushiol herb with the largest following is Jewelweed, also known as Touch-Me-Not or Impatiens. It is a common wetland plant frequently found in the company of *Toxicodendron*. You can't miss the pale yellow or yellow-orange spurred flowers that hang like jewels with ripe seedpods that explode at the slightest touch.

The effectiveness of this plant as Poison Ivy/Poison Oak palliative is not equal to its reputation. There is no scientific evidence extant that Jewelweed juice is any better or worse than the sap of Plantain, the common garden and lawn weed, or the liquor of Aloe used for burns and bruises, or any of the many herbs touted as *Toxicodendron* tamers. The best that can be said for these herbs is that some may relieve the itching for a time but they are ineffective in turning the *Toxicodendron* tides despite sworn testimony of ardent advocates to the contrary.

Water Treatment for Urushiol Dermatitis

In spite of the myriads of medications for the rhus rash, experts suggest the simplest, least expensive and most effective treatment is gallons and gallons of just plain running cold water. Since the oily resins containing urushiols are only slightly soluble in water, a little water spreads the venom and a lot flushes it away.

Out-of-doors do not hesitate to wash in the waters of swamps, brooks, lakes, rivers, canteens, or the juice of wetland plants which usually have succulent stems that exude liquid when broken. "Go jump in a lake" may not be a bad advice to urushiol hypersensitive unfortunates. Better to be soaked than sorry.

Regardless whether or not you wash the affected areas outdoors, plan to spend some time under a cold shower as soon as possible to rid yourself of any clinging oily residues that can spread and contaminate other parts of the body. The sooner and longer you shower, the better are the chances of avoiding or at least minimizing a rash.

There was a time not so long ago when a strong, brown laundry soap, Fels Naphtha to be exact, was considered the soap of choice, the unquestioned preventive of the rash. However, old fashioned suds or modern bath soaps have been found to be poor solvents for urushiols. In fact, soaps, moisturizers, oils (palm, olive, and coconut), combine with urushiols and spread them.

In addition, soaps and detergents also remove natural oils that protect the skin against urushiol penetration. Since it takes several hours for these oils to regenerate, another contact with urushiol, in the interim, could cause a more severe rash than previously. Hence, soap is not recommended nor warm water which quickens urushiol absorption. The soapless, cold water treatment appears to be a more effective approach to eliminate or minimize the itchy bumps and blisters of urushiol dermatitis.

Time is of the essence; the sooner you start the cold water treatment, the better. The more sensitive you are, the less time there is before the urushiols are absorbed and set the rash mechanism in motion. "Exquisitely sensitive" individuals have very little time, minutes, in which to wash away the ominous oils. After that, such hypersensitive persons are resigned and wait for the rash to appear. According to Dr. William Epstein, who has been studying West Coast Toxicodendrons for the past 30 years, individuals with average sensitivity have a grace period of 2 to 3 hours. In view of the many factors that influence the onset and severity of the rash, this may be an overestimate. To be on the safe side, get under a cold shower as soon as possible.

Steroids

If, in spite of all prescribed precautions, the rash begins to raise its itchy, red, inflamed head, there still is hope. Modern science has produced drugs that have the reputation of turning the tide and halting the progress of the rash. The miracle medications are the *steroids*; as a gel or cream, they work wonders when rubbed into the skin if the affected area is limited and in the early stages of mild or moderate rash eruptions. Don't expect a "quick fix." Severe cases are treated with steroids under medical supervision. However helpful high potency steroids are, they are not a sure cure for everybody, but are the best now available.

A good part of the dermatitic damage is self-inflicted by scratching, which disrupts the healing process and invites secondary infections. Short of declawing and tying the hands of rash sufferers behind their backs, anti-itching medications are applied to prevent these victims from skinning themselves alive. A widely used preparation is *calomine lotion,* which lessens the itching and absorbs blister liquid in mild cases but does not stop the rash. Cold compresses with Burrow's Solution (aluminum acetate, an astringent), oatmeal baths (one cup to a tub of water), and aspirin are recommended home treatments to relieve the itch. Severe rashes may require medical attention and intervention. In general, before resorting to self-treatment of the rash with home remedies or off-the-shelf pharmaceuticals or both, it is advisable to see a physician.

"Catching" Dermatitis

One of the most persistent myths about urushiol dermatitis is that it is "catching." Some innocents believe that the liquid, oozing out of the blisters contains the rash-causing poison and therefore you can "catch" the rash by coming in contact with a urushiol victim or the blister liquid.

This fiction was disproved over two centuries ago by Thomas Horsfield, previously mentioned, who accepted the "evil effluvium" theory but rejected the "poison-blister-fluid" myth. He is credited with performing one of the earliest immunological experiments with Poison Ivy and came to the following conclusion:

"I ... attempting to propagate it [Poison Ivy dermatitis] by inoculating with the serous fluid contained in the vescicle [blisters]; but in no instance was I able to excite the infection."

Horsfield repeated this investigation with several people highly sensitive to Poison Ivy and got the same results each time. Since this landmark discovery, other investigators have verified Horsfield's findings, namely, that the liquid in the Poison Ivy blister is not infectious, contagious, or toxic. The real culprits are the urushiols that initiate the rash; the disseminators of the rash may be the sufferers themselves. They spread the unabsorbed oils lodged on the skin or under the fingernails by scratching or touching other parts of the body or anybody or anything. Keeping fingernails short minimizes scratching and the source of urushiol reinfection.

10

CONTROLLING TOXICODENDRONS

THEORETICALLY, the ultimate solution to the *Toxico-codendron* problem is their total annihilation. However, a program of "Toxicodendricide" is neither practical nor desirable as this would in all probability produce an ecological vacuum creating more problems than it solves. A more realistic approach is to find ways and means of controlling and confining these poisonous weeds, especially in heavily populated residential or recreational areas and school sites.

There are two strategies that can be deployed to contain and tame *Toxicodendron*. One is hand-to-hand combat and the other chemical warfare. The tactic in the direct field offensive is to seek out and liquidate the "enemy" completely, the entire plant, subterranean roots and stems, surface stolons, aerial vines, flowers and fruits. Keep in mind that the "opponent" is a woody perennial capable of regenerating from bits and pieces. Dismembering the fallen foes and leaving them on the battlefield, may create more opponents than are killed. Also, be aware that these wily weeds can launch a chemical counterattack long after they have been cut to pieces. Don't underestimate the power of Toxicodendrons to give a good account of themselves in the struggle to survive.

"T-Day" ground offensives should be planned for moist, cool days in early spring or late fall when these adversaries are leafless and hence armed with the least amount of their chemical weapon, urushiol. It is also much easier to dislodge the underground portions of these plants from wet soil than from hard, dry ground.

The proper "battle fatigue" is clothing that gives complete cover, including thick leather or cotton gloves (not rubber) for hands-on encounters. Once again, do not assume you are safe from enemy "fire" based on past performance. Attack climbing vines by cutting them at the base and removing the urushiol-loaded aerial vines, but handle with care. The rooted portion, which may be too difficult to unearth, will probably sprout leaves at the cut end the following spring. Manual grubbing alone, especially with well established growths, is usually not enough.

This calls for the second strategy, chemical warfare using herbicides as ammunition to eliminate Toxicodendrons. These plant killers are usually fired by sprayers at a safe distance for the operator. Recommended herbicides include amitrole, silvex, ammonium sulfamate, 2-4D, 2-4DP, and triclopyr. They are sold under their common names as well as various trade labels. "Poison Ivy and Poison Oak Killer" is one such preparation which contains triclopyr as active ingredient. The safest is ammonium sulfamate, Ammate, which on the one hand breaks down to ammonium sulfate, a harmless fertilizer, and on the other hand, acts as a broad-leaf plant killer that injures any plant it touches. Furthermore, it must be applied repeatedly before it destroys the weed.

No matter which herbicide you choose, be sure to read the small print on the label and follow the manufacturer's directions exactly. If used according to directions, a herbicide will go a long way in eliminating Toxicodendrons; otherwise it can be a disaster, particularly when Poison Ivy or Poison Oak is entwined with valuable plants.

Herbicidal offensives are best conducted on windless days in the late spring when the Toxicodendrons display the greatest amount of foliage and therefore the maximum damage can be inflicted upon their exposed "flanks." After two or three aerial bombardments, the leaves turn yellow and drop off, and the stems and roots are mortally wounded. The attack should be aimed against the invader only; otherwise innocent bystanders will also be casualties.

There is a problem in disposing of *Toxicodendron* corpses that are full of urushiols. The one thing you don't do is cremate the remains. The "winds of war" may shift and urushiol-bearing smoke particles may rain down on the incendiary and turn success into bitter biting defeat with a rash that covers every exposed part of the body and inflames the mouth, nasal passages, and lungs.

"Bag and bury" in your own back yard or land fills, using biodegradable bags, appears to be the best way to dispose of *Toxicodendron* remains. But don't assume that by winning one battle against Poison Ivy you have won the war. Birds may drop seeds in the very area that was cleaned out and once again the battle is on. However, whether you pull, pinch, or spray, when the campaign against *Toxicodendron* is over, unless the weapons, uniforms, and soldiers are washed free from all traces of urushiol, it will be a Pyrrhic victory for rash-bearing combatants. Finally, when all else fails, hire a flock of goats and let them loose in a field of Poison Ivy or Poison Oak. In time, considering their voracious and omnivorous appetites, they will eat these plants out of existence.

Bag and bury is the preferred way to dispose of *Toxicodendron* remains. Make certain that biodegradable containers are used.

11

IN PRAISE OF TOXICODENDRONS

THE TALE of the Toxicodendrons would be incomplete without mentioning the virtues and values of Poison Ivy and its close relatives. Although there are those who see these plants as incorrigible botanical Borgias, accomplished poisoners that do away with their enemies, others see them in a more favorable light as respectable, praiseworthy, useful members of the botanical kingdom.

There is much speculation as to the function of the urushiols for the plant. One view holds that these chemicals have survival value and that their toxicity provides protection against hordes of hungry microbes, insects, and many herbivores that would otherwise feed on these plants.

Another supposition is that the resinous oils are self-sealing substances that plug and disinfect breaks and bruises and so prevent microbes from invading and infecting injured plants. This may account for the general good health of Toxico- dendrons.

Others believe urushiols are normal products of plant meta- bolism whose precise role is one of the many "secrets" still to be unraveled.

Then there are the rash victims who take a strictly anthro- pomorphic stance and insist that the venom is directed against humans. More seriously and still in the realm of investigation is how, when, and why some people become urushiol sensitive and others do not.

Uses of Urushiols

Long before Columbus opened the doors to America, the native Indians from coast to coast were familiar with the virtues and vices of the Toxicodendrons. Indian braves called them "bad women" and the squaws agreed that these plants were "sticks that make you sick." These herbs were greeted with "you are my friend" either as a declarative or interrogative statement depending upon how well the bearer of this salutation got along with them.

The earliest published reference to native Poison Ivy and its uses appeared in 1635 in *History of the Plants of Canada*, a treatise by Jacques Cornut (1606-1651) who was a Parisian physician. This work, the first botanical account of North American flora, contains an excellent illustration and detailed description of Poison Ivy, probably *T. rydbergii*, with the comment that the milky sap is used as a hair dye. No mention is made of who used it or what the effects were on the user.

A few years later, in 1678, John Banister (1650-1692), an English cleric and America's first resident botanist, cataloged the flora of the Virginia colony. This publication states that the plant "Poysinweed," also called "Virginia Dye Tree," derives its name "from the qualities of its juice which on linnen turnes black and will not loose its color in the wash, with it our negroes mark their shirts."

American Indian Folklore

Pacific Northwest Indians wove baskets from the supple slender stems of *T. diversilobum* and used the juice to blacken the basket fibers in ornamental designs. The twigs were used to split salmon and smoke it over a fire. The leaves were mixed with acorn meal to make bread and also to cover meat and other foods while baking. It is quite remarkable that edibles, flavored with the urushiol oils, were consumed without ill effects or so the story goes. To bring good luck while gambling, the Navahoes chewed a small piece of Poison Ivy leaf and shared it with an opponent.

Poison Ivy *(Edera trifolia Canadensis)*. The illustration is an adaptation of the first published drawing of Poison Ivy that appeared in Jacques P. Cornut's *History of Canadian Plants,* 1635. He named it *Edera trifolia Canadensis,* Three-leaved Ivy of Canada.

American Indian medicine men believed in the curative powers of the Toxicodendrons. Seeds of Northern Poison Ivy,

T. rydbergii, were included in their medical pouches. In the west, the sap of *T. diversilobum*, Western Poison Oak, was applied to warts, ringworm, and snake bites. Northeastern tribes crushed the root of Poison Ivy and applied it as a poultice to sores, swollen glands, boils that had to be opened and drained, and as a "disinfectant" to open wounds. Also, the bark of Poison Oak served as a powerful emetic. An infusion made from the leaves of Poison Ivy was taken as a rejuvenating spring tonic.

Poison Sumac, *T. vernix*, was the Cherokee medicine man's herb of choice against chills, asthma, fevers, gonorrhea, mucus discharges, tuberculosis, ulcers, ulcerated bladders, and any other illness requiring "strong" medicine.

The many tales about the immunity of native American Indians to the ravages of the Toxicodendrons are contradicted by the reported recipes and practices for treating the rash. The Algonquins rubbed Poison Ivy on Poison Ivy rashes. Mohegans treated the rash with a boiled mixture of dry corn cobs and the leaves of Poison Oak, *T. toxicarium*. Oklahoma Delaware Indians made a salve from Poison Oak leaves and placed it on the affected area. West coast tribes made a tea from the leaves of *T. diversilobum* and drank it to acquire immunity. These stories and others cannot be verified and remain in the realm of Indian folklore.

From all accounts, Indians used a variety of herbs to prevent and treat *Toxicodendron* rashes; included were Touch-me-not, Pennyroyal, Gumweed, Milk Vetch, Shepherd's Purse, Mountain Mint, Vervain, and Dogwood. Again, documentation as to their effectiveness is lacking.

Modern Medicine

The great skill and "know how" of Indians were not lost on white settlers, their physicians and pharmacists. They applied Toxicodendrons with equal success and failure in the treatment of skin diseases such as eczema, erysipelas, shingles, and warts. The homeopathic approach of Indians, treating urushiol rashes with urushiol, has not lost its place in modern medical practice. Several well known commercially prepared medications for the prevention and treatment of urushiol dermatitis contain urushiol extracts from Poison Ivy, Poison Oak, and Poison Sumac in various combinations. How much more effective these modern pharaceuticals are than the crude Indian treatments is worth considering.

Soil Stabilizer

The extensive underground woody stoloniferous systems of poison ivies and poison oaks are ideal for stabilizing the soil. *T. radicans* grows abundantly in huge patches along the sandy shorelines of Long Island, southern New York, and New Jersey, where it has helped to keep the beaches from washing away. The Dutch have planted poison ivies on their earthen dikes and succeeded in keeping the soil in and diggers out. On the West Coast, their role as an effective agent for erosion control on the "shaky hills" of California has not been overlooked.

A rather unusual use of Poison Ivy is to construct hedge-rows from it. To keep intruders out and apples in his orchard, a farmer planted fences of Poison Ivy and reported some success in discouraging "apple snatchers."

Tribute to the Toxicodendrons

The Toxicodendrons are not without honor except in their own land, where they are feared and shunned as "untouchables" by the uninitiated and ill-informed. As early as the 1640's French and English adventurers and explorers were carting off shiploads of North American plants that were welcomed in the gardens of Europe. The Toxicodendrons were included in spite of their "evil" reputation. Abroad they were admired not only as New World "exotics" and conversation pieces, but also for their intrinsic beauty especially in the fall when they are most colorful. Poison Ivy went along to New Zealand and New South Wales where it is alive and well.

Recently, a rumor was spread that there grew in the famous Chelsea Physic Garden in London, a nonpoisonous form of Poison Ivy. Correspondence with the Director of the Garden put an end to this tale of the "tamed" *Toxicodendron*. He added the story of the American student who collected an exquisitely colored trifoliate vine growing in the Garden. A day later when the class met, the student was as red as the specimen of Poison Ivy, a victim of the urushiol rash. Whether home or abroad, Poison Ivy is Poison Ivy bringing pain to some pleasure to others.

And yet, the Toxicodendrons do have friends and admirers. Some daring gardeners and knowledgeable horticulturists have planted and propagated Poison Ivy and Poison Oak as ornamentals. Although this is not a common practice in this country, it has gained more acceptance abroad as previously mentioned.

A most compelling reason for joining the "Society for the Preservation and Protection of Toxicodendrons" is ecolological. These plants are an integral part of the delicately balanced web of life, which we are systematically and continuously upsetting to the detriment of all living things including ourselves.

Growing in all directions, up, down, and around, poison ivies and poison oaks from coast to coast have created domains that provide food, shelter, and protection for a multitude of animals. Bees find nectar and honey in the sweet smelling *Toxicodendron* flowers; a vast variety of birds feed on the berries; large mammals such as bears, cattle, deer, goats, hogs, horses, and sheep eat the stems and leaves without a single reported case of dermatitis or gastritis. Small mammals—rabbits, squirrels, rodents, and others- subsist on the berries and seeds. The thickets of these plants provide cover that protect burrowers from predators and us.

All in all, the Toxicodendrons are no less important for human survival than other members of the plant kingdom. Their contributions far outweigh the damage they inflict upon unwary urushiol-sensitive individuals.

The poison ivies and poison oaks from coast to coast join other weeds in concealing the ugly scars and wounds we inflict, and the rubbish and rubble we heedlessly dump upon the earth. Festooning living and dead trees and shrubs, Toxicodendrons delight the eye and add color to the fall foliage festival. Above all, these plants have "bravely" battled soil erosion. All that remains is for us to learn how to live in peaceful coexistence with them. Although there is much we do not know about Toxicodendrons, there is hope that in time we will better understand and appreciate them. To paraphrase Abraham Lincoln:

Mother Nature must have loved the Toxicodendrons,
She made so many of them.

Appendix A

THE TEN TOXICODENDRON TENETS

1. Thou shalt not be ignorant of the Toxicodendrons and their parts all the days of the year.

2. Thou shalt not touch or cause to be touched Toxicodendrons and their parts all the days of the year.

3. Thou shalt not touch or cause to be touched animals and objects that have touched Toxicodendrons all the days of the year.

4. Thou shalt not destroy Toxicodendrons by fire for the smoke will fall upon thee and thine eyes and poison thee.

5. Thou shalt not expose thine limbs to Toxicodendrons but cover thine nakedness against their venom.

6. Thou shalt not be arrogant and say thou hast immunity from Toxicodendrons all the days of thine life.

7. Thou shalt not tarry but immediately cleanse thineself of the touch of Toxicodendrons by washing with cold water.

8. Thou shalt not treat the Toxicodendron rash visited upon thee by tearing at thine flesh for it inflicts further pain and suffering.

9. Thou shalt not believe that the liquids that ooze from the blisters of this affliction causeth it to spread on thine body and the body of thine friends and neighbors.

10. Thou shalt not look upon Toxicodendrons as an enemy for they are a blessing to many creatures of the earth and the earth itself.

Appendix B

Key to
Some Common Native Species of
Toxicodendron and *Rhus*

I. Fruits axillary, drooping, ivory to white: ***Toxicodendron***

    A. Leaflets 3

        1. Leaflets coarsely toothed to entire; fruits hairless

            a. Vine or shrub; aerial roots
                Climbing Poison Ivy, *T. radicans*

            b. Shrub; no aerial roots; Northern habitat
                Nonclimbing Poison Ivy, *T. rydbergii*

        2. Leaflets lobed or entire

            a. Vine or shrub; leaflets smooth; West coast
                Western Poison Oak, *T. diversilobum*

            b. Shrub, hairy; East coast
                Eastern Poison Oak, *T. toxicarium*

    B. Leaflets more than 3

        1. Leaflets 7-13, edges entire, pinnate; wetland
                Poison Sumac, *T. vernix*

II. Fruits terminal, upright, red to brown: ***Rhus***

    A. Leaflets 3

        1. Leaflets hairy, fragrant when crushed; rare
                Aromatic Sumac, *R. aromatica*

    B. Leaflets more than 3, pinnate

        1. Leaflets sharply toothed

            a. Branches covered with dense brown hairs
                Staghorn Sumac, *R. typhina*

            b. Branches hairless, shiny
                Smooth Sumac, *R. glabra*

        2. Leaflets entire, soft downy; rachis winged
                Winged Sumac, *R. copallina*

Appendix C
Suggested Books and Periodicals

Baker, S. 1979. *Poison Oak and Poison Ivy*. Author, Soquel, California.

Benson, A.B. (Ed.) 1966. *Peter Kalm's Travels in North America*. Dover Press, New York.

Cronin, E. 1980. *Contact Dermatitis*. Church and Livingston, Edinburgh, Scotland.

Crooks, D.M. and D.L. Klingman, 1977. *Poison Ivy, Poison Oak and Poison Sumac*. U.S. Department of Agriculture, Farmer's Bulletin 1972, Washington, D.C.

Elias, T. 1980. *Trees of North America*. Van Nostrand Reinhold, New York.

Epstein, W.L. and V. Byers. 1981. *Poison Oak and Poison Ivy Dermatitis*. U.S. Department of Agriculture, Forest Service, Missoula, Montana.

Fernald, M.L. 1970. *Gray's Manual of Botany*. 8th ed. Van Nostrand Reinhold, New York.

Fisher, A.A. 1986. *Contact Dermatitis*. 3rd ed. Lea and Febiger, Phila., Penn.

Gillis, W.T. 1971. The Systematics and Ecology of Poison-Ivy and the Poison-Oaks (Toxicodendron, Anacardiaceae). *Rhodora*, **73** (793-796):72-540.

————— 1975. Poison Ivy and its Kin. *Arnoldia*, **35**(2):93-123.

Kingsbury, J.M. 1968. *Poison Ivy, Poison Sumac, and other Rash-Producing Plants*. New York State College of Agriculture, Cornell University, Cornell Extension Bulletin 1154, Ithaca, New York.

Lampe, K.F. and M.A. McMann. 1985. *AMA Handbook of Poisonous and Injurious Plants*. American Medical Association, Chicago, Illinois.

Leite, D. 1982. *Don't Scratch*. Weathervane Books, Walnut Creek, California.

Mitchell, J.C. and A. Rook. 1979. *Botanical Dermatology*. Greengrass, Vancouver, Canada.

Mitchell, J.D. 1990. The Poisonous Anacardiaceae Genera of the World. *Advances in Economic Botany*, **8**:103-129.

Rostenberg, A. 1955. An Anecdotal Biographical History of Poison Ivy. *AMA Archives of Dermatology*, **72**:438-445.

Schwartz, D.M. 1986. Leaflets Three. *Country Journal*, **12**(8):42-50.

Shepherd, S. 1990. The Scourge of the Great Outdoors: Poison Ivy and Poison Oak. *Executive Health Report*, **26**(8):2-3.

Vietmeyer, N. 1985. Science has got its Hands on Poison Ivy, Oak and Sumac. *Smithsonian*, **16**(5):89-95.

Winterringer, G.S. 1963. *Poison Ivy and Poison Sumac*. Illinois State Museum, Story of Illinois Series, No. 13, Springfield, Illinois.

INDEX